47 Beautiful Ideas Created with
Succulents, Air Plants, Moss and Orchids

# Decorative Terrariums

Sueko Katsuji

# A miniature world of plants, enclosed in clear glass

The world's first terrarium was created in London in the 19th century. It was used for growing plants and rearing insects and small animals. The natural environment created in the box enabled plants to survive transportation for long distances, and carried out an important role in life.

I opened my shop, Buriki no Zyoro, in the midst of a small boom about terrariums. Nowadays, lots of containers and other goods for terrariums can be found on the market making it even easier to enjoy terrariums. Rather than simply arranging plants inside a terrarium, there are now many original and fun ways for enjoying terrariums such as choosing unusual containers, or combining various kinds of dry materials such as driftwood or cork.

I began to incorporate moss and orchids after I started writing this book. The fleshy roots and bulbs of orchids have something in common with succulents that is appealing. With moss, I have tried to recreate in the terrarium the scenery I saw when I visited the mountains of the Kiyosato area in Japan. I hope you will be able to sense the mysterious yet strong elements of moss.

As long as you know certain techniques, anyone can easily make a terrarium. You don't need a special container. You could start with something already in your household, such as storage jars or even candle holders. The deserts or the jungles you can see through the glass are full of life enabling plants to adapt to that environment, miniature as it may be. If this book enlightens readers as to how interesting terrariums and plants are, then I shall be very happy.

Sueko Katsuji, Owner of Buriki no Zyoro

# Contents

# ulent plants

## Chapter 1

The long watering cycle and slow growth rate of succulents

makes them well suited to terrariums.

One way to enjoy them is to grow a variety of shapes and textures.

We can make a world with a natural landscape by combining them

with other materials.

# no.01

## Pale green succulents seen in light filtering through lace curtains

A hanging type of terrarium, so cute no matter what angle it is viewed from. When hanging near a window, avoid direct sunlight by using lace curtains.

1. *Haworthia cooperi* 2. *Sedum* cv. Alice Evans
3. *Crassula* cv. Blue Bird 4. Aqua soil 5. Bark chips
Container: A drop-shaped terrarium container
(φ 6.7in/170mm × H 6.7in/170mm)

**1**

In the bottom of the container place some material to prevent root rot together with bark chips. Put chips on the very bottom so that it looks nice when viewed from below.

**2**

Place a small amount of soil in the container. Plant some *Haworthia cooperi* in the back of the container using tweezers. Get rid of soil on the plant's roots before putting it in the container.

**3**

In front of the *Haworthia cooperi*, plant the *Sedum* cv. Alice Evans and *Crassula* cv. Blue Bird.

**4**

Finally, put aqua soil in the spaces in between using a spoon or similar tool.

—— point ——

Because the hole of the container is narrow, plant only a few succulents to make maintenance easy. Complicated arrangements are not a good idea.

# no.02

## Small glass domes for displaying as part of home décor

A good method of display for succulents that have been cut and the roots have not yet grown again, or are still short. It's possible to change the plants according to your mood, and you can have fun with these as part of your home décor.

1. *Pachyveria* cv. Blue Mist 2. *Echeveria* cv. Pallida Prince 3. Palm fiber 4. Peat moss 5. *Graptopetalum paraguayense*
Container: Glass domes
(W 16.1in/410mm × D 5.5in/140mm × H 7.9in/200mm)

**1** Take the *Pachyveria* cv. Blue Mist out of its pot and lightly brush the soil off its roots. Then wrap the roots up in peat moss.

**2** Wrap the palm fiber around the peat moss so that it is all covered up. Do the same with the other succulents.

**3** Staple the palm fiber in four places to firmly attach it. Be careful not to damage any of the succulent roots with the staples.

—— *point* ——

As the glass domes are airtight, peat moss and palm fiber are used instead of soil so that the succulents can breathe better. Replant the succulent if roots appear on it.

*succulent plants*

# no.03

## Cacti play the main role in a compact group of various plants

Grouping together cacti that don't grow very tall, in a small petri dish. Creating a landscape with cork looking like rock.

1. *Huernia* 2. *Echinocereus rigidissimus* subsp. *rubispinus* 3. *Frailea* 4. *Notocactus scopa* var. *ruberrimus* 5. Cork 6. Soil mix
Container: Petri dish
(φ 4.3in/110mm × H 3.5in/90mm)

| | | |
|---|---|---|
| In the bottom of the petri dish put in some material to prevent root rot and then the soil. Position the cork. | Take the largest cacti, the *Huernia*, from its pot and using tweezers and a brush, plant it beside the cork. | With an eye to the entire balance, plant the three other smaller cacti. Smooth the soil over with the brush after planting. |

*point*

The good thing about cacti is that they like heat and are easy to grow in summer and in winter indoors. Open the lid to the petri dish once a day for a change of air.

14

## A fun parallel combination that looks like paintings

Two narrow rectangular terrarium containers placed side by side. Changing the depth of the soil the position of stones and soil when viewed from the side. Make full use of your imagination in creating these terrariums.

1. *Graptopetalum* cv. Snow White 2. *Echeveria* cv. Shimo-no-Ashita 3. [Right] *Sedum rubrotinctum*, [Left] *Graptopetalum* cv. Bronze 4. *Sedum rubens* 5. Soil mix 6. Pumice stone 7. *Echeveria* cv. Takasago-no-okina 8. *Crassula mesembryanthemoides* Container: Narrow rectangular terrarium containers (W 4.7in/120mm × D 2.0in/50mm × H 4.7in/120mm)

**1**

In one of the containers put in some material to prevent root rot, followed by pumice stones, and soil mix. Use the tweezers to plant *Graptopetalum* cv. Snow White on the right side.

**2**

Plant the *Crassula mesembryanthemoides* as though it were grass, and then plant *Echeveria* cv. Takasago-no-okina on the left side.

**3**

Use a funnel to fill in the spaces left over with soil. Make a funnel by rolling up a clear plastic folder.

**4**

In the other container, place some Iceland moss (*Cetraria islandica*) to create a deep layer and last of all, use a brush to smooth the soil. Using a brush creates a natural look.

---
*point*
---

In small terrariums like these, water the plants using a narrow nozzle to reach the plants' roots. Take care not to spatter and dirty the container while watering the plants.

---

*succulent plants*

# no.05

## Enjoy layering different kinds of soil in a jar from your kitchen

Only in glass terrariums can you enjoy the colorful layers of soil and sand. Use the metal clamp of the jar to prop the lid open.

1. Pumice stone 2. Bark chips 3. *Rhipsalis cassutha*
4. Sand 5. Iceland moss
Container: Storage jar
(φ 4.3in/110mm × H 9.8in/250mm)

**1** Place some material to prevent root rot in the bottom of the jar. Follow with layers of sand, pumice stone, Iceland moss and bark chips.

**2** Take the *Rhipsalis* out of its pot and using a pair of tweezers, plant it in the jar. Put bark chips around it to hide the roots and soil.

*succulent plants*

# no.06

## Hanging *Rhipsalis* upside down

Using a hyacinth jar for an arrangement of *Rhipsalis* hanging upside down. After the hyacinth flowers are finished, why don't you try using the jar this fun way?

1. Peat moss 2. Iceland moss 3. *Rhipsalis pilocarpa*
4. Fishing line
Container: Hyacinth jar
(φ 3.9in/100mm × H 7.9in/200mm)

Take the *Rhipsalis* out of its pot and wrap peat moss around its roots.

Wrap Iceland moss around the peat moss and tie it up with fishing line.

Wrap paper around the *Rhipsalis* to prevent damage and put it through the part of the jar where the bulb usually sits. Take the paper off and put the plant in the jar. Water by soaking the moss part directly in water.

## A simple terrarium in a coffee pot

Containers in the kitchen can be used for terrariums.
A terrarium in a coffee pot is just right for
decorating the dining table or a kitchen shelf.

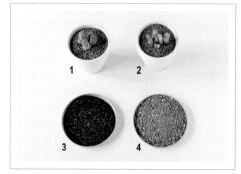

A : [Right] *Lithops julii* subsp. *fulleri*, [Left] *Lithops schwantesii* 2. *Ophthalmophyllum* 3. Rice husk charcoal 4. Soil mix (with a large ratio of rice husk charcoal mixed in)
**Container: Coffee pot**
(φ 4.3in/110mm × H 7.9in/200mm)

**1**

Place material to prevent root rot, and rice husk charcoal in the bottom of the pot.

**2**

Next add the soil mix and plant the succulents. *Ophthalmophyllum* tends to break up easily so take care when pushing it in.

**3**

Use a funnel for filling in the spaces with soil mix and avoid getting soil on the succulents.

———— *point* ————

*Lithops julii* subsp. *fulleri*, *Lithops schwantesii* and *Ophthalmophyllum* are winter hardy succulents so do not water too much but change watering frequency according to the season. In summer, water once every two weeks and in winter, about once every five days.

## *Haworthia* in a rectangular terrarium

A group planting of five types of *Haworthia*, one of the more translucent kind of succulent plants. Positioning the plants to match the curvature of the branch.

1. Branch 2. *Astroloba bullulata* 3. *Haworthia turgida*
4. *Haworthia cooperi* var. *pilifera variegata* 5. Soil mix
6. *Haworthia* cv. Yumedono 7. *Haworthia truncata*
8. *Haworthia cooperi*
Container: Case for terrariums
(W 18.1in/460mm × D 5.9in/150mm × H 5.9in/150mm)

Put the branch in the terrarium case. Choose a branch that is curved, not straight.

Spread material to prevent root rot, and soil mix in the case. Plant the *Haworthia cooperi* var. *pilifera variegata* slightly to the right of the center.

Plant the other succulents keeping the placement in mind. Planting the *Astroloba bullulata* close to the *Haworthia cooperi* var. *pilifera variegata* will balance out the arrangement.

After planting everything, bury the roots firmly by putting extra soil mix in the spaces between the succulents.

— point —

*Haworthia* should be watered more than other succulents. Aim to water once every five days. Water directly after planting too.

*succulent plants*

# no.09

## Enjoying succulent plants that grow vertically

This simple terrarium uses only peat moss and cork, not soil. As it doesn't use soil, it can be placed anywhere, which is good.

1. *Senecio stapeliiformis* 2. *Cissus cactiformis*
3. Peat moss 4. Fishing line 5. Cork
Container: Flower vase
(φ 5.5in/140mm × H 11.8in/300mm)

**1**

Take the *Cissus cactiformis* out of its pot and wrap the roots up in peat moss. Place cork around this and secure it with fishing line.

**2**

Place cork in the base of the flower vase so that the plants' roots do not come in direct contact with the glass. Arrange large pieces of cork in the vase too.

**3**

Do the same with *Senecio stapeliiformis*. Position the succulents in the vase to achieve a good balance.

*succulent plants*

# no.10

## A dynamic yet simple terrarium

This type of terrarium has the succulent plant as center of attention. Having plants to the side, rather than the center, creates asymmetrical impression. The container is suited to low tables or for placing on the floor.

1. Soil mix 2. *Argenteo* 3. *Echeveria cante*
Container: Flower vase
(φ 9.8in/250mm × H 9.1in/230mm)

**(1)**

Spread material to prevent root rot, and soil mix in the vase. Take the *Echeveria cante* from its pot and plant it off-center, to the side.

**(2)**

Plant the *Argenteo* around the *Echeveria cante* to set it off. Use a nozzle to water the plants so that no water gets spilt on the leaves.

—— *point* ——

The white powder on the leaves of *Echeveria cante* will come off if you touch it or if water gets on the leaves. Be careful.

*succulent plants*

# no. 11

## Recreating a desert landscape in a tilted terrarium

Instead of using a glass cover vertically as intended, this terrarium uses it tilted diagonally. The terrarium is stabilized by placing it in the lid of a petri dish, cushioned with palm fiber.

1. *Pachyphytum* cv. Gekkabijin 2. *Echeveria shaviana*
3. *Crassula mesembryanthemoides* 4. *Kalanchoe pumila* 5. *Echeveria* cv. Rezry 6. *Sedum* cv. Sunrise Mom 7. Soil mix 8. Sand
Container: Glass cover
(φ 5.5in/140mm × H 5.9in/150mm)

**1**

First, decide the angle for tilting the container and stabilize it. Spread material to prevent root rot, and soil, and make it level in the container. Rope coiled up can be used as the base for the terrarium.

**2**

Take the *Pachyphytum* cv. Gekkabijin out of its pot and plant it in the center using tweezers.

**3**

Plant the *Echeveria shaviana*, *Crassula mesembryanthemoides*, *Kalanchoe pumila*, *Echeveria* cv. Rezry, and *Sedum* cv. Sunrise Mom starting from the back. Lastly, finish off the arrangement by adding sand.

—— *point* ——

When using a container tilted to one side, be careful when putting the soil inside. Make sure it lies flat and is not tilted at an angle when planting the succulents in the container.

# no. 12

## A square terrarium placed diagonally to enjoy from different angles

This container that looks like it is tilted diagonally has a bold presence. While taking care with the balance in volume, make a terrarium that also has depth.

1. *Chamaecereus silvestrii* 2. *Crassula lycopodioides* var. *pseudolycopodioides* 3. *Kalanchoe rhombopilosa* 4. *Sulcorebutia rauschii* 5. Mt. Fuji sand 6. Soil mix 7. Branches of mulberry trees
Container: Cubic terrarium container
(W 5.9in/150mm × D 5.9in/150mm × H 5.9in/150mm)

Spread material to prevent root rot, and then soil mix blended with 10% of Mt. Fuji sand (the coarse composition promotes good drainage) in the container.

Take the *Chamaecereus silvestrii*, which takes up more space than the others, from its pot and plant it in the front, low down. Then plant the *Sulcorebutia rauschii* up behind it.

Position the mulberry branches and plant the *Kalanchoe rhombopilosa* beside the *Sulcorebutia rauschii*.

Divide the *Crassula lycopodioides* var. *pseudolycopodioides* into two and plant the two plants in different places. Lastly, use the funnel to spread Mt. Fuji sand on the surface.

___ point ___

When using a container tilted diagonally, be careful to make the soil lie flat. Positioning plants that take up the most space in the front, will achieve the best balance overall.

# no.13

## Creating a snowy scene in monotone with sand and cacti

*Cereus spegazzinii* f. *cristatus* take center role here. The white fuzz around its areoles are reminiscent of snow. The chic monotone tints of these cacti suit the dryness of the sand.

**1.** *Astrophytum ornatum* **2.** *Euphorbia mammillaris*
**3.** *Cereus spegazzinii* f. *cristatus* **4.** Sand
**Container: A terrarium case in the shape of a house**
**(W 8.3in/210mm × D 5.1in/130mm × H 8.7in/220mm)**

Spread material to prevent root rot, and sand in the bottom of the case. Take the *Cereus spegazzinii* f. *cristatus* from its pot and plant slightly on an angle, while keeping balance in mind.

Using tweezers, plant the *Astrophytum ornatum* in the center and then the *Euphorbia mammillaris* beside it.

Brush off any sand on the cacti and then give the sand some natural curves and ups and downs with the brush.

___ point ___

Sand that drains well is good for terrariums but it tends to lack nutrients. Supplement this with some diluted fertilizer occasionally.

*succulent plants*

no.14

## Bonsai inside a glass dome

A stone container for bonsai is used inside a glass dome. Just one plant combined with the texture of the container creates various ways to enjoy a terrarium.

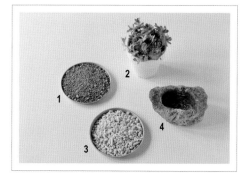

1. Soil mix 2. *Orostachys genkaiense* 3. Coral
4. Pumice stone for bonsai
Container: Glass dome combined with wooden base
(φ 7.9in/200mm × H 9.8in/250mm)

Place soil mix in the pumice stone container and then plant the *Orostachys genkaiense* in it.

Arrange the runners of the *Orostachys genkaiense* so that it fits in the pumice stone.

Arrange coral in the bottom of the glass container and then on top of the coral, place the pumice stone container with the plant in it. Finish by placing the glass container on the wooden base.

_____ *point* _____

As the *Orostachys genkaiense* is sitting in a pumice stone container with excellent drainage, material to prevent root rot is not necessary.

succulent plants

no. **15**

## A fun arrangement of *Dorstenia hildebrantii crispum* of different heights

The natural atmosphere of a pale wood container is complemented by the textures of stone and coral. Enjoy the different heights of *Dorstenia hildebrantii* f. *crispum* in this clever arrangement with its swathes of unused space.

1. *Pseudolithos migiurtinus* 2. *Tephrocactus articulates* f. *diadematus* 3. *Dorstenia hildebrandtii* f. *crispum* 4. Stone 5. Soil mix 6. Coral
Container: Terrarium container made of pale wood and glass (φ 7.5in/190mm × H 10.6in/270mm)

Spread material to prevent root rot, and soil mix in the container. Place the stone off-center, near the outer side.

Take the three *Dorstenia hildebrantii* f. *crispum* out of their pots and plant them in a triangular composition, keeping in mind the balance with the container.

Plant the *Pseudolithos migiurtinus* and *Tephrocactus articulates* f .*diadematus* in front of the stone. Lastly, spread coral on top of the soil.

_____ point _____

When planting more than one of the same variety of succulent, it is easy to get the balance right if you plant the biggest or tallest one first.

33

## Four types of *Sempervivum* in a group planting

This is a group planting of succulents that are dormant in summer and grow in winter. Consider the balance with the driftwood when laying it out so that it looks beautiful from above too.

1. Driftwood 2. *Sempervivum* cv. Lipari
3. *Sempervivum* cv. Glaucum Mirror 4. *Sempervivum* cv. Red Chief 5. *Sempervivum arachnoideum* 6. Soil mix 7. Stone
**Container: Canister
(φ 7.5in/190mm × H 10.2in/260mm)**

**1**

After looking at the driftwood and deciding how it will be placed, put it in the center of the canister.

**2**

Spread material to prevent root rot, and some soil mix in the bottom of the container. Position the stone taking the overall balance into consideration.

**3**

Using tweezers, plant the succulents in the spaces between the driftwood and the stone.

**4**

Taking care that the soil doesn't cover the succulents, use the funnel to fill in the spaces with soil. Take the lid off once a day for a change of air.

*point*

Succulent plants that are dormant in summer and grow in winter need different care to those that grow in summer. So it is better to plant groups of the same kind and not mix them. They don't like a lot of moisture so do not water too much.

# air plants

## Chapter 2

Air plants, in their pastel shades,

are often used in home décor.

Their unique form gives rise to various shapes,

growing straight or even curly.

Air plants are very light and aerial in feeling.

So if they are placed curling around a branch,

they give terrariums a three-dimensional feel.

air plants

# no. 17

## Enjoy creating a display using some plain bottles

A casual arrangement using bottles from the kitchen for storing spices or cereals. You can change the contents or increase the number of bottles. The cork lids provide an accent.

1. Nuts 2. *Tillandsia harrisii* 3. Stones 4. *Tillandsia fuchsii* 5. Small branch 6. Iceland moss
Container: Bottles with cork lids
(φ 3.1in/80mm × H 8.3in/210mm)

(Bottle on left-hand side of photo)

**1**

Put stones and nuts in the bottom of the bottle. Place Iceland moss on top using tweezers.

**2**

Insert the branch at an angle.

*point*

Leave the lid off for a while once a day for a change of air. Putting other things than plants inside the bottles and displaying them together is fun too.

**3**

Use tweezers to place the *Tillandsia harrisii* at the foot of the branch.

**4**

Hang the *Tillandsia fuchsii* higher up on the branch.

# no.18

## Mixing air plants with cut succulents

Succulents and air plants together in a candle holder. Display by hanging up or sitting on a shelf. Evoke a sense of movement with a vine.

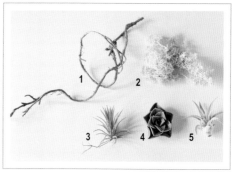

1. Vine (*Hedera rhombea*) 2. Iceland moss 3. *Tillandsia ionantha* 4. *Echeveria* cv. Perle Von Nürnberg
5. *Tillandsia harrisii*
Container: Candle holder
(φ 3.9in/100mm × H 6.7in/170mm)

**1**

Put Iceland moss in the bottom of the candle holder. Insert the *Hedera rhombea* through the hole in the lid.

**2**

Use tweezers to insert the *Tillandsia harrisii* from the side. Curl the *Tillandsia ionantha* around the vine. Last of all, place the *Echeveria* cv. Perle Von Nürnberg inside the container too.

air plants

# no.19

## A hanging lamp with greenery floating out

Entwine greenery in the socket of a lamp not used anymore. The curvy lines of *Tillandsia usneoides* create a soft impression.

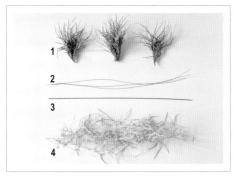

1. *Tillandsia bandensis* 2. Fine wire 3. Thick wire
4. *Tillandsia usneoides*
Container: An old lamp
(φ 5.9in/150mm × H 8.7in/220mm)

Wind the fine wire around the roots of three strands of *Tillandsia bandensis* and form a clump.

Insert the clump into the socket part of the lamp and secure it with thick wire.

Wind the *Tillandsia usneoides* around ②. Cover this all with the glass shade. Watering can be done with the socket in place.

air plants

no. 20

## Fresh greenery,
## just right for the kitchen

Air plants are put in a large lemonade jar, in a three-dimensional manner to create a miniature botanical garden. Display in the kitchen or in the dining room.

1. *Tillandsia juncifolia* 2. Branch 3. *Tillandsia fasciculata* 4. Iceland moss 5. Driftwood chips
6. *Tillandsia fuchsii* 7. *Tillandsia stricta* 8. *Tillandsia gardneri* 9. Wire
Container: Lemonade jar
(φ 7.1in/180mm × H 12.2in/310mm)

Put Iceland moss and the driftwood chips in the bottom of the lemonade jar. The moss only needs to be seen here and there, not all over.

Secure the *Tillandsia gardneri* in the middle of the branch with wire, then put the branch in the jar leaning against the side.

Place the *Tillandsia juncifolia, stricta, fuchsii* and *fasiculata* in the jar starting with the largest one first. Position them paying attention to overall balance.

___ point ___

Air plants like *Tillandsia gardneri* which do not have their roots exposed are better suited to hanging in the air.

## A natural arrangement using some coral

The air plants that appear to have some movement are placed in the holes in the lump of coral to achieve a natural landscape. The coral was chosen because of its bumpy shape.

1. *Tillandsia juncea* 2. *Tillandsia loliacea* 3. *Tillandsia usneoides* 4. Twigs 5. Sand 6. *Tillandsia bulbosa*
7. *Tillandsia reichenbachii*
Container: A dome-shaped terrarium
(φ 7.1in/180mm × H 7.1in/180mm)

Spread sand in the plate and then place the lump of coral on it as though it was a garden rock.

Wrap the roots of *Tillandsia reichenbachii* in peat moss and put hot bond on the moss, then glue it into a groove in the coral.

Place the twigs near the edge and position the *Tillandsia juncea, loliacea, usneoides,* and *bulbosa* around the coral so that it is all well balanced.

— *point* —

The way to show the overall balance properly is to combine different sizes of air plants, big and small. Don't make a front and a back but make it pleasant to view from any angle.

air plants

# no.22

## A three-dimensional arrangement using dried banana stems

Banana stems refers to dried banana stalks of the flowers, known as the peduncle. The stalks protrude from the beaker on purpose, to draw attention to the vertical line. The true form of the plant is recreated.

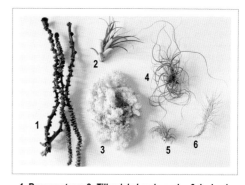

1. Banana stems 2. *Tillandsia brachycaulos* 3. Iceland moss 4. *Tillandsia butzii* clump 5. *Tillandsia ionantha* 6. *Tillandsia caerulea*
Container: Beaker (φ 7.1in/180mm × H 12.6in/320mm)

Put a layer of Iceland moss in the bottom of the beaker so the plants are not sitting directly on the glass.

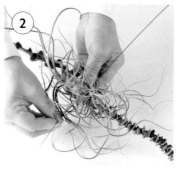

With wire, secure the *Tillandsia butzii* clump in the middle of a longish banana stem.

Including the banana stem from ②, put four stems in the beaker. Then place *Tillandsia brachycaulos, ionantha* and *caerulea* at the foot of the banana stems.

_____ point _____

For watering, take the plants out each time and spray them with water. Return them to the container when they are completely dry. The plants wired to the banana stem can be sprayed with water as is.

47

no.23

A lampshade that looks like a painting when casually positioned

A lampshade used in a tilted position.
The curly air plants and the aerial cauliflower roots create a light image.

1. *Tillandsia utriculata* clump 2. *Tillandsia pseudobaileyi* 3. *Tillandsia tricolor* var. *melanocrater*
4. Cauliflower roots
Container: Lampshade
(W 8.3in/210mm × D 8.3in/210mm × H 8.3in/210mm)

Decide on how you want to place the lampshade and spread out the cauliflower roots inside starting from the back.

Using tweezers, place the *Tillandsia utriculata* clump and *Tillandsia tricolor* var. *melanocrater* in the back.

Add the *Tillandsia pseudobaileyi* by placing on top. Some of the leaves can protrude from the lampshade.

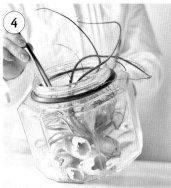

Using the tweezers, adjust the position of the air plants amongst the cauliflower roots, to stabilize them.

—— point ——

If it is difficult to obtain cauliflower roots, you can substitute shells or white twigs instead.

# no.24

## Air plants made to look like seaweed —a combination of materials

Just *Tillandsia caerulea*, with its unique form, is combined with other various materials. An image reminiscent of the ocean floor is created.

1. *Tillandsia caerulea* 2. Stones 3. Branches 4. Dried mushrooms 5. Dried Spanish moss 6. Board
Container: A case for storing key-holders
(W 11.0in/280mm × D 3.1in/80mm × H 7.1in/180mm)

**1** Stand the board up at the back of the case. The metal parts for key-holders are part of the terrarium and do not need to be hidden.

**2** Spread dried Spanish moss here and there on the bottom of the case. Place the stones and branches at random.

**3** Using tweezers, place seven pieces of *Tillandsia caerulea* in one place. Make it look as though they grow from there and have branched off.

—— *point* ——

Decide the position for making the most of the lines created by the *Tillandsia caerulea* as it grows straight up. Making them all anchored in the same place, instead of here and there, gives a natural look.

*air plants*

# no.25

## *Tillandsia streptophylla* and a base that looks like stones in a garden

Putting some stones one on top of another creates some spaces in the container. Ventilation is good making a comfortable terrarium for the plants.

1. *Tillandsia juncea* 2. *Tillandsia reichenbachii*
3. *Tillandsia streptophylla* 4. Stones
Container: Flower vase
(φ 8.3in/210mm × H 6.7in/170mm)

**①** Place the three large stones in the vase so they are one on top of the other. Using driftwood in a three-dimensional way instead of stones will create the same well-ventilated space.

**②** Put the *Tillandsia reichenbachii* and *Tillandsia streptophylla* in between the stones. So that they will face sideways, insert them on an angle.

**③** Lastly, use the tweezers to insert the *Tillandsia juncea*. Its leaves can protrude from the top of the vase.

*air plants*

# no.26

## A terrarium with a bunch of dried flowers

Adding the dried flowers makes the colors stand out, looking almost like a bouquet. This makes a lovely gift.

1. *Sarracenia* 2. *Protea* 3. *Tillandsia ionantha*
4. *Tillandsia funckiana* 5. *Fatsia japonica berries*
Container: A long, narrow terrarium
(φ 5.5in/140mm × H 11.8in/300mm)

**1** Use the long, narrow terrarium container by laying it down, not standing up. First, put in the *Protea*, the largest dry flower.

**2** Using the tweezers, put the *Fatsia japonica berries* and the *Sarracenia* on top of the *Protea*.

**3** At the bottom, put in the *Tillandsia funckiana* and up the top, place the flowers of the *Tillandsia ionantha*.

# MOSS

## Chapter 3

Rather than a sunny aspect,

moss prefers a bright yet shady place.

Moss is easy to display indoors

and can be enjoyed regardless of the season.

After a generous watering,

the way droplets of water spread out under the glass is beautiful.

no. 27

## A round kokedama for simply enjoying the charm of moss

Making a kokedama may seem difficult, but it is just enclosing a ball of soil in moss. Easier than you would imagine. The round shape is so cute. Have fun making it!

— point —

Aqua soil is of good quality and well suited to making kokedama. Take the lid off the container sometimes for a change of air.

1. Aqua soil 2. *Brachymenium exile* 3. Fishing line
Container: Canister (φ 3.5in/90mm × H 6.7in/170mm)

Mix some water into the aqua soil in a bowl and then form a round ball. This is the base of the kokedama.

Place *Brachymenium exile* all around the ball, completely enclosing it.

Wrap fishing line around the entire ball to secure the moss and finish the ball.

Place material to prevent root rot, and aqua soil in the bottom of the canister. Then place the kokedama on top of that.

# no.28

## Layers of material for viewing sideways

Placing the bottle on its side is a great idea. It looks beautiful from the side, and you can make layers that drain well. Peeping in through the mouth of the bottle is fun too.

1. *Conocephalum conicum* 2. *Sagina subulata*
3. Bark chips 4. Cryptomeria bark 5. *Brachythecium populeum* 6. Kanuma soil
Container: Storage jar
(W 5.1in/130mm × D 5.1in/130mm × H 7.1in/180mm)

Place the jar on its side and first put in material to prevent root rot, and Kanuma soil. Using tweezers, spread out the Iceland moss.

Make layers using the bark chips and cryptomeria bark, until they reach as high as the middle of the container.

Using tweezers, place *Conocephalum conicum* in the back of the container.

Place *Brachythecium populeum* around the *Conocephalum conicum* and towards the front of the container.

Using two different kinds of moss with different shape leaves gives this terrarium an interesting look. Spray with water and enjoy watching how the droplets spread out in the container.

— *point* —

Cryptomeria bark is from a mountainous environment and is a good base material that is suited to moss. It also has the effect of maintaining appropriate levels of moisture in the terrarium.

moss

# no.29

## Miniature worlds that make you want to look closer

These small hanging terrariums are a popular item in our shop. Enjoy using them to decorate a small space like a bay window or front entrance.

1. Cryptomeria bark 2. *Dionaea muscipula*
3. *Dicranales*
Container: Hanging vase
(φ 4.7in/120mm × H 4.7in/120mm)

Spread material to prevent root rot, and cryptomeria bark in the base of the hanging vase. Remove the *Dionaea muscipula* from its pot and plant it with tweezers after removing excess soil from its roots.

Spread out the *Dicranales* from the back to the front and lastly, gentle press it down with the tweezers.

# no.30

## A bonsai-style terrarium with a Japanese black pine

A kokedama with the roots of a Japanese black pine, a popular tree for bonsai. The crispness of Japanese style seen through glass is something novel and fresh.

1. Cryptomeria bark 2. *Pinus thunbergii* (Japanese black pine) 3. *Hypnum plumaeforme Wilson* 4. Stones
Container: A tall dome-shaped terrarium
(φ 5.5in/140mm × H 10.2in/260mm)

**(1)** Remove the Japanese black pine from its pot and lightly brush off the soil from its roots. Wrap cryptomeria bark around its roots to protect them.

**(2)** Enclose the roots wrapped in bark with *Hypnum plumaeforme Wilson*, making a round ball.

**(3)** Wrap black string around the ball and adjust the shape if necessary. Place on top of the stones on the plate.

_____ point _____

Kokedama dry out very easily so the best method is to soak it in water and let it absorb lots of water. Water once every two days (depending on the season).

# no.31

## Keeping an eye on *Pyrrhobryum dozyanum* as it grows upwards

As *Pyrrhobryum dozyanum* will grow taller a flask that has leeway vertically was chosen. Pieces of wood, not cork, for the lid give a natural accent.

1. Aqua soil 2. Stones 3. *Pyrrhobryum dozyanum*
4. *Lemmaphyllum microphyllum*
Container: Conical flask
(φ 6.7in/170mm × H 11.0in/280mm)

**1** Place material to prevent root rot, and aqua soil in the bottom of the flask.

**2** Using the tweezers, position the two stones in the center.

—— *point* ——

Sometimes the leaves of the *Pyrrhobryum dozyanum* turn yellow. Prune the tips when they start to change color.

**3** Plant the *Lemmaphyllum microphyllum* in front of the stones and press it down lightly to anchor the roots.

**4** Place the *Pyrrhobryum dozyanum* on the opposite side and plant the roots firmly.

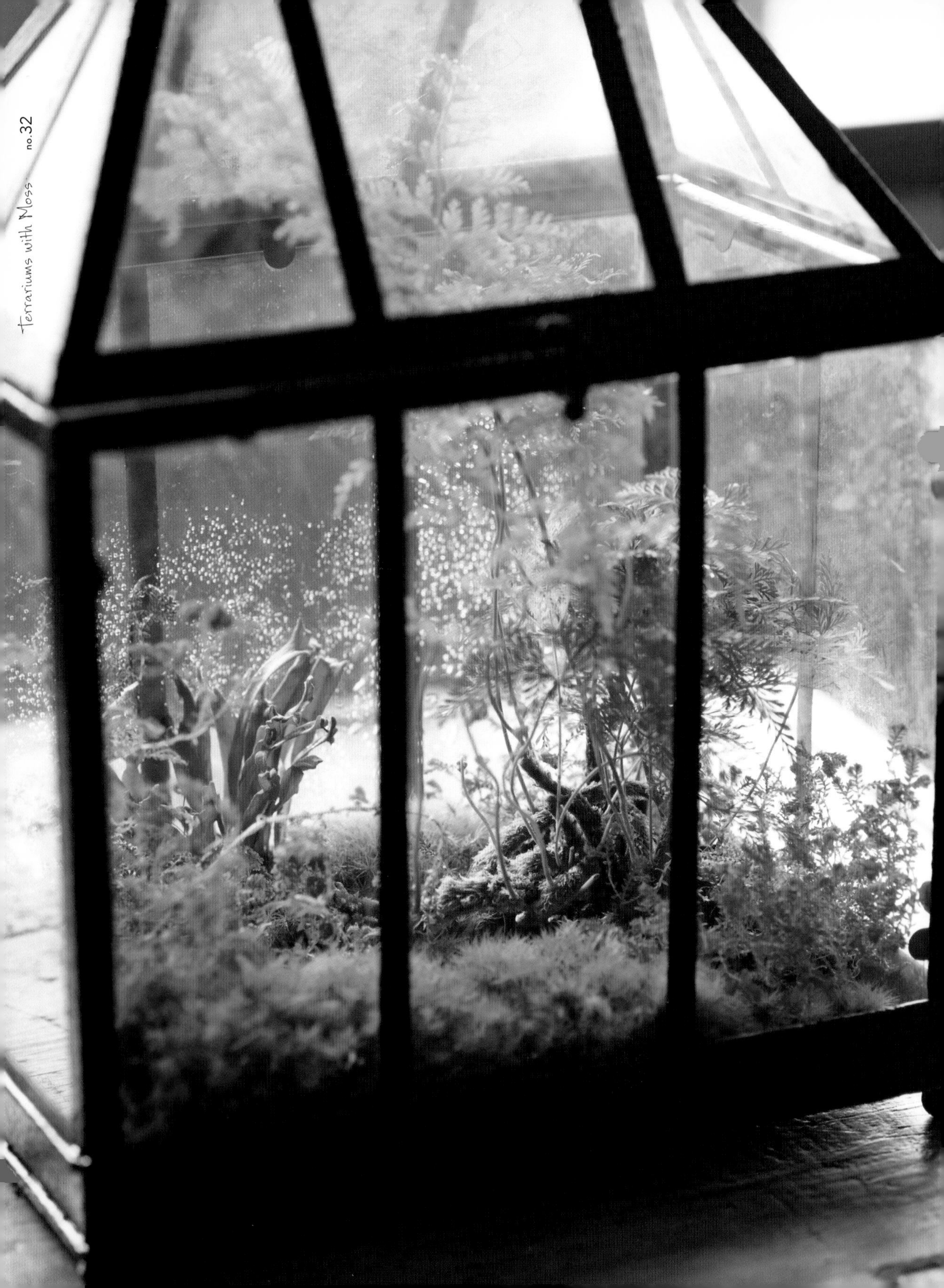

# no.32

## A tiny jungle that makes you feel a breath of life

A lush jungle-like atmosphere is created by using various types of moss and ferns of different heights. This tiny world looks like something may be living in it.

1. *Davallia fejeensis* 2. *Pyrrosia davidii* 3. *Selaginella remotifolia* 4. Aqua soil 5. *Bartramia pomiformis*
Container: A terrarium in the shape of a house
(W 12.6in/320mm × D 8.7in/220mm × H 16.5in/420mm)

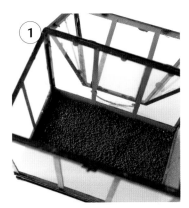

Place material to prevent root rot, and aqua soil in the bottom of the container.

Remove the *Davallia fejeensis* from its pot and plant it with the soil still attached to its roots.

*point*

Keeping a natural environment as the image you are aiming for, create a landscape where the base of the ferns is covered with moss. Placing the *Davallia fejeensis* in the center and then the other plants around the edges in the container creates a natural landscape.

Plant the *Pyrrosia davidii* in the same way taking care to balance it out, and plant the *Selaginella remotifolia* near the *Davallia fejeensis*.

Plant the *Bartramia pomiformis* in between to fill in the spaces. Open the lid sometimes for a change of air.

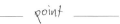

# no.33

## Enjoying the different textures of *Nepenthes* and moss

The insectivorous plant *Nepenthes* goes well together with moss. A landscape with humidity that seems almost tropical is created inside the glass container.

1. Aqua soil 2. *Hypnum plumaeforme* 3. *Nepenthes*
Container: A drop-shaped terrarium container
(φ 5.1in/130mm × H 8.7in/220mm)

**1**
Place material to prevent root rot, and aqua soil in the bottom of the container. Remove the *Nepenthes* from its pot and plant it.

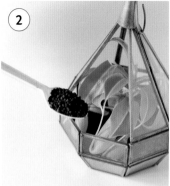

**2**
Use a tool like a spoon to add more aqua soil and bury the roots properly.

**3**
Spread out the *Hypnum plumaeforme* using tweezers. If the leaves of the *Nepenthes* turn brown, cut them off at the base of the leaf.

# no.34

## Different species of plants that coexist in nature

As time went by, moss gradually grew on the *Orostachys japonica*.
A weed grew there too and they were transplanted in their natural state.

1. Aqua soil 2. *Pottiaceae* (with *Orostachys japonica* growing on it)
Container: A multi-faceted terrarium container
(W 6.3in/160mm × D 6.3in/160mm × H 6.3in/160mm)

**1**

Place material to prevent root rot, and aqua soil in the bottom of the container.

**2**

Take the *Pottiaceae* together with the *Orostachys japonica* out of the pot and plant as is, in one piece.

**3**

Taking care not to get soil on the plants, use a spoon to spread aqua soil around the plants to hide their roots.

# no.35

## Casual terrariums using bottles from your kitchen

An arrangement for enjoying two kinds of moss by placing the tall bottle on its side. Also fun to view from above by placing the bottle underneath a glass table.

1. *Racomitrium canescens* 2. *Pyrrosia lingua*
3. Kanuma soil 4. *Marchantia polymorpha*
Container: Bottle with a lid
(W 12.2in/310mm × D 5.5in/140mm × H 3.9in/100mm)

**1**

Place material to prevent root rot, and Kanuma soil in the bottle. To prevent any damage, place the *Racomitrium canescens* on a ruler or similar tool and slide it in to the far end of the bottle.

**2**

Make a small depression in the Kanuma soil and using tweezers, plant the *Pyrrosia lingua.*

**3**

Plant the *Marchantia polymorpha* in front of the *Pyrrosia lingua*. For watering, aim for the back of the bottle when spraying to ensure that droplets of water reach all over.

MOSS

# no.36

## An arrangement in an oil bottle that looks good in the kitchen

*Nephrolepis* is divided up and put in an olive oil bottle with moss. This slim bottle will fit in a small corner of the kitchen.

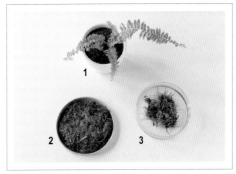

1. *Nephrolepis* 2. Cryptomeria bark
3. *Brachythecium populeum*
Container: Olive oil bottle
(φ 3.9in/100mm × H 11.8in/300mm)

Place material to prevent root rot, and cryptomeria bark in the bottle. Take the *Nephrolepis* from its pot and after brushing off the soil, plant it using tweezers.

Spread *Brachythecium populeum* around the *Nephrolepis*. The mouth of the bottle is narrow so inside will retain its moisture even with the lid off.

no.**37**

A combination of *Adiantum* and a branch with moss growing on it

If you find a branch with moss growing on it, make up a new terrarium. *Adiantum* is popular because of its attractive foliage, and when used like this, it creates a different atmosphere.

1. Cryptomeria bark 2. *Leucobryum bowringii Mitt.*
3. *Adiantum* 4. Branch (with moss attached to it)
**Container: Antique glass bottle**
(W 5.5in/140mm × D 3.9in/100mm × H 12.2in/310mm)

Place material to prevent root rot, and cryptomeria bark in the bottle. Take the *Adiantum* from its pot and plant it after brushing off some of its soil.

Using tweezers, plant the *Leucobryum bowringii Mitt.* so that it looks like a little mountain in the bottle.

Push the branch inside the bottle so that it is at an angle.

Use a branch short enough to be able to close the lid on the bottle.

_____ *point* _____

For a terrarium with moss in a bottle with a wide mouth, the lid should be kept on the bottle. Water by spraying everything in the bottle. In doing this, the air will be changed too.

# no.38

## An arrangement that focuses on the vertical lines of *Sarracenia*

*Sarracenia* is a plant that grows in damp ground, so it goes well with moss. Using a container that sets off the vertical line gives a sharp impression.

1. *Sarracenia* 2. *Leucobryum juniperoideum*
3. **Kanuma soil**
**Container: A tall terrarium container**
**(W 5.1in/130mm × D 5.1in/130mm × H 11.8in/300mm)**

Place material to prevent root rot, and Kanuma soil in the container.

Take the *Sarracenia* from its pot with the soil still attached, and plant it in the container, using tweezers. Position it firmly in the Kanuma soil.

Place the *Leucobryum juniperoideum* in the container, starting from the back. Make it thickly covered with the moss all over.

___ point ___

This can be said for all mosses—they should be generously watered directly after planting. Then the moss will absorb the water and become firmly established.

75

# no.39

## Using a Japanese dish and coral to produce a Japanese gardenscape

Simply by using a pottery plate, a terrarium can take on a Japanese feeling. The piece of coral looks like a garden stone. This terrarium suits a Japanese-style room or a wooden corridor.

1. *Davallia mariesii* 2. Coral 3. Cryptomeria bark
4. *Thuidium* 5. *Brachythecium plumosum*
6. *Leucobryum bowringii Mitt.*
Container: Pottery plate and glass dome
(φ 7.1in/180mm × H 10.6in/270mm)

**1**

In the plate, spread material to prevent root rot, and cryptomeria bark that has been wetted with water.

**2**

Position the coral and spray all over to moisten.

**3**

Take the *Davallia mariesii* from its pot and after gently brushing off some soil, plant it on the coral and fixing it in place by pressing down lightly.

**4**

Spray the *Thuidium* and *Brachythecium plumosum* with water and then plant them on the coral, fixing them in place by pressing down lightly, as in ③. Plant the *Leucobryum bowringii Mitt.* around the coral.

**5**

Using tweezers, push the small *Brachythecium plumosum* into depressions in the piece of coral. Lastly, spray well all over with water. Place the glass dome on top.

*point*

When affixing plants to stone or coral, the important thing is to choose a piece that has various depressions on it. The grainy surface makes it easier to attach the moss and will make it look as though the moss grows there naturally.

# orchids

## Chapter 4

The elegant flowers gain much attention focused on orchids.

But terrariums show off their thick leaves and bulbous roots.

Orchids are said to be the slowest to develop out of all plants.

They attach themselves to trees and have the knack

of being able to live in lots of different places.

They grow well in containers too.

# no.40

## Using a container effectively to show the cuteness of small orchids

Touches of pink in white flowers, the focus here is a small orchid close to the original species. The teardrop-shaped container, that reflects light in complex ways, suits this arrangement well.

1. Bark chips 2. *Hypnum plumaeforme Wilson*
3. *Dendrobium kingianum*
Container: A teardrop-shaped container for terrariums
(φ 6.3in/160mm × H 11.4in/290mm)

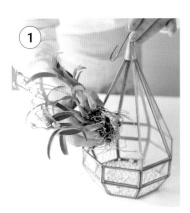

**1** Spread material to prevent root rot in the bottom of the container. Take the *Dendrobium kingianum* from its pot and gently brush soil off the roots. Then position it in the container.

**2** Cover the surface inside the container with bark chips. Bury the roots of the *Dendrobium* properly by spreading the chips thickly.

**3** Then spread the *Hypnum plumaeforme Wilson* on top of that, using tweezers. Hang indoors in a bright place but avoid direct sunlight.

--- *point* ---

The moss spread out around the orchid will retain moisture well. Do not overwater but only water when the soil is completely dry.

orchids

# no.41

## Two different colored *Paphiopedilum* that would make a lovely gift

The orchids placed amongst the ruffled *Selaginella remotifolia* look very sweet in this arrangement. Wrapped up in wax paper and tied with hemp twine, it would be a lovely gift.

1. *Paphiopedilum* (green) 2. *Paphiopedilum* (red)
3. *Selaginella remotifolia* 4. *Hypnum plumaeforme Wilson* 5. Peat moss 6. Bark chips
Container: Canister
(φ 7.9in/200mm × H 15.0in/380mm)

**1** Spread material to prevent root rot, and bark chips in the bottom of the container.

**2** Take the two *Paphiopedilums* out of their pots and gently brush soil off the roots. Then wrap peat moss around the roots and plant them in the container.

**3** Take the *Selaginella remotifolia* out of its pot and divide into three.

**4** Gently brush soil off the roots and wrap peat moss around them. Using tweezers, plant in three places around the *Paphiopedilums*.

**5** Fill in the spaces by planting *Hypnum plumaeforme Wilson*. Cover the mouth of the container with wax paper that has air holes in it.

____ point ____

The orchid family has many with distinguishing features. *Paphiopedilum* are not epiphytes but terrestrials so we can enjoy them planted in a container.

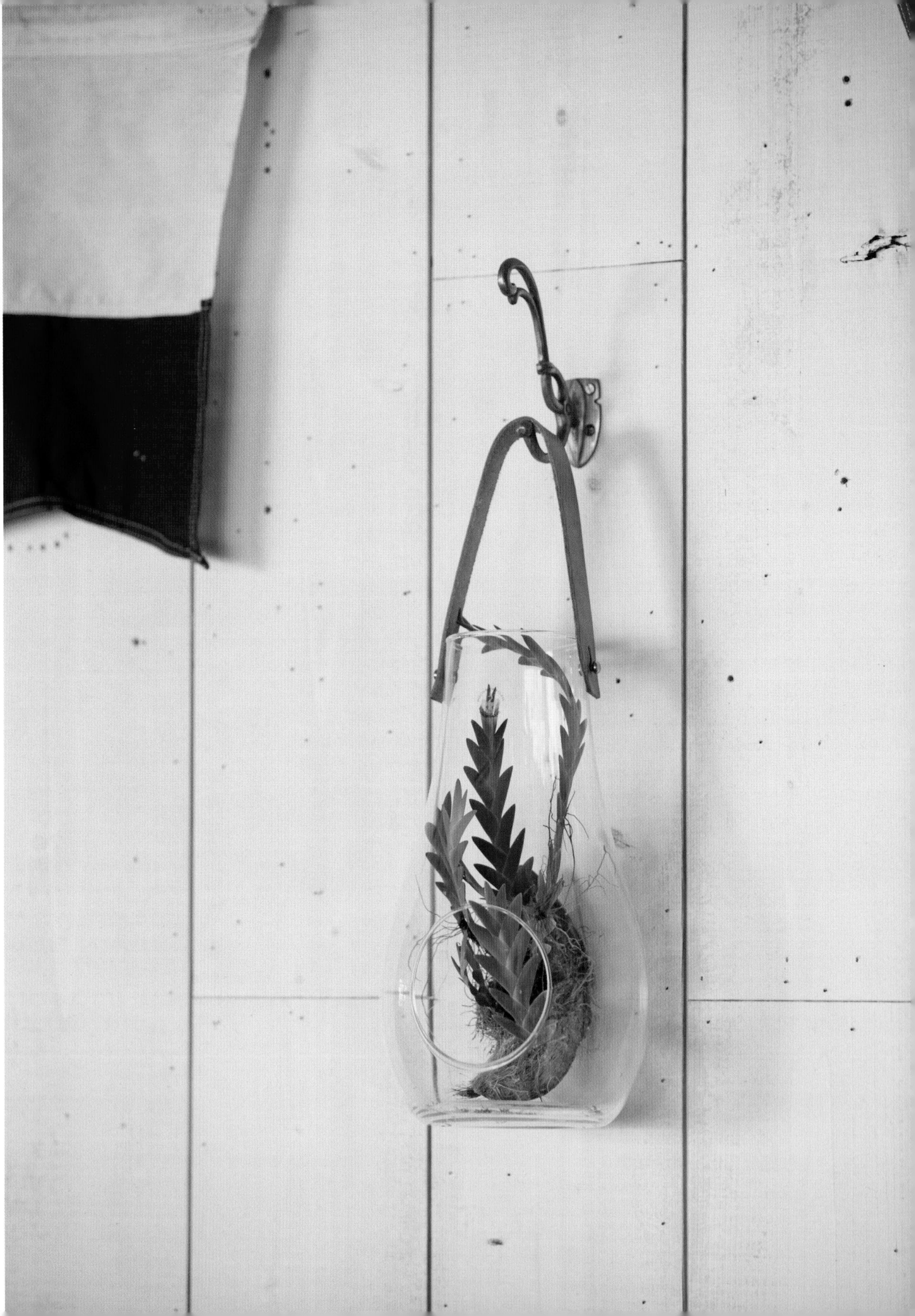

# no.42

## Enjoy the unusual qualities of this orchid in a candle holder

This species, with its fleshy leaves similar to succulents, is quite popular. After attaching the roots to the coconut husk, it is displayed casually in a hanging candle holder.

1. Coconut husk 2. *Eria aporoides* 3. Hemp twine
4. Peat moss
Container: Candle holder
(φ 5.9in/150mm × H 11.4in/290mm)

**1** Take the *Eria aporoides* out of its pot and brush the soil off its roots. Then wrap peat moss around them.

**2** Soften the inner fibers of the piece of coconut husk by pulling on them.

**3** Attach the *Eria aporoides* from ①. To the piece of coconut husk by wrapping hemp twine around it. Then place the final product inside the candle holder.

—— point ——

Wrap peat moss densely around the base of the roots, not just the tips. This stabilizes the roots and also retains moisture.

# no.43

## Different kinds of orchids hanging and placed on the floor of this terrarium

Inside the one terrarium two types are being grown, hanging and placed on the floor. This arrangement is quite large so it could be put in the living room as central display.

1. *Angraecum didieri* 2. *Dendrochilum* 3. Cork
4. Peat moss 5. Wire 6. Hemp twine
Container: A terrarium in the shape of a house
(W 8.3in/210mm × D 5.5in/140mm × H 9.8in/250mm)

(1)

In one of the pieces of cork, make two holes in the top of the cork and put a piece of wire through it.

(2)

On the side of that piece of cork, make two more holes and put through a piece of hemp twine to tie the *Angraecum didieri*.

(3)

Take the *Angraecum didieri* out of its pot and take off the old peat moss. (Cut any roots that have changed color.)

(4)

Use the hemp twine to tie the *Angraecum didieri* from ③ to the cork.

(5)

Wrap the wire attached to the cork to the top of the terrarium container and hang ④. Attach the *Dendrochilum* to a piece of cork in the same way and place it on the bottom of the container covered with other pieces of cork.

_____ point _____

Take the *Dendrochilum* from its pot and wrap all the roots in peat moss properly. Enable it to grow on the cork by attaching it with wire.

# no.44

## A simple arrangement for enjoying the roots of *Phalaenopsis*

If you want to include *Phalaenopsis* in a casual way, this method is good. Try this using some leftover orchids, not those specially made up for display.

1. *Midi Phalaenopsis* 2. A wooden frame with the kind of mesh used in the bottom of pots 3. Peat moss
4. Hemp twine
Container: Flower vase
(φ 7.1in/180mm × H 19.7in/500mm)

**1** Remove the *Midi Phalaenopsis* from its pot and remove the soil (bark chips) on the roots.

**2** Prune any roots that have gone black and leave only healthy roots.

**3** Wrap peat moss around the roots securely for retaining moisture, getting rid of whatever moss falls off naturally.

**4** Put the plant in the wooden frame with mesh wrapped around it and tie it securely with the hemp twine. Put this final product in the flower vase and display accordingly.

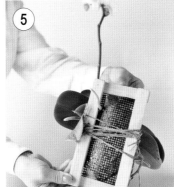

**5** The mesh provides good ventilation and the roots will become entwined in the mesh as they grow.

___ *point* ___

For watering, take the wooden frame in its entirety out of the vase and spray with water. Return to the glass vase when it is dry.

# no.45

## Using a pasta storage jar for an easy and fun terrarium

Attaching three orchids randomly using the crevices in the cork. The trick here is to balance the arrangement well so it can be enjoyed from any angle.

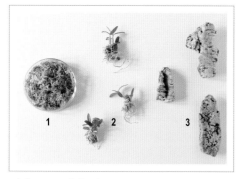

1. Peat moss 2. *Dendrobium* cv. Proud Appeal 3. Cork
Container: Pasta storage jar
(φ 3.9in/100mm × H 11.8in/300mm)

**1** Join two or three pieces of cork together using hot bond to make a long narrow base.

**2** Take the three *Dendrobiums* from their pots and wrap peat moss densely around their roots.

**3** Use a staple gun to attach the peat moss to the cork. Place the finished cork arrangement in the canister. Each plant only needs to be attached in one or two places. Take care not to damage the roots when using the staple gun.

orchids

# no.46

## A wooden case to display in a study

*Masdevallia ignea*, also called "Princess Tears" evokes the image of a fairy. This mature arrangement is in a black wooden case. Display along with antiques, or in a study perhaps.

1. Peat moss 2. *Hypnum plumaeforme Wilson*
3. *Masdevallia ignea* 4. Black thread
Container: Display case
(W 6.7in/170mm × D 6.7in/170mm × H 16.5in/420mm)

**1** Take the *Masdevallia* out its pot and brush off excess soil around the roots. Wrap the roots in peat moss.

**2** Wet the *Hypnum plumaeforme Wilson* and wrap it around the orchid's roots that are wrapped in peat moss. Finish by winding black thread around the entire ball. Display inside the case.

# no.47

## A primitive scene
## using a natural piece of wood

Using a branch with *Hedera hibernica* vine wrapped around it. The aim is to make the most of the natural shape so it is okay to have it poking out in a dynamic fashion.

1. *Dendrobium* cv. Angel Baby 'Green Ai' 2. *Oncidium splendidum* 3. Wooden frame 4. *Oncidium miltonia* 5. *Hypnum plumaeforme Wilson* 6. Peat moss 7. Hemp twine 8. Branch with moss attached to it
Container: Display case
(W 9.4in/240mm × D 9.4in/240mm × H 18.5in/470mm)

*point*

Use the same method to attach *Oncidium miltonia* higher up on the branch. Including another branch with *Oncidium splendidum* attached to it in the same way will give a feeling of depth to the composition.

Take the *Dendrobium* from its pot and removed the old peat moss that the roots are attached to.

Wrap new peat moss around the roots which have been tidied up.

Use hemp twine to tie the roots of ② to the wooden frame.

Use *Hypnum plumaeforme Wilson* to hide the twine wrapped around the roots. Using moss makes it look as though the orchid is growing naturally.

succulent plants

air plants

moss

orchid

# Chapter 5

Basics of Terrariums &
Encyclopedia of Plants and Flowers

Merits of terrariums include being able to make a
terrarium with simple steps, that they fit in with
any kind of interior decor, and they make it easy to
include plants into your everyday life.
This chapter will introduce points on basic ways to
make a terrarium, explain how to water and look
after terrariums, and about containers and tools, and
also includes a Q&A corner.
The final section has an encyclopedia of plants and
flowers suited to terrariums.

## point

# Points for Making Beautiful Terrariums

Terrariums are miniature worlds
created by using all the elements in a container.
Once you know certain knacks, you can devise
various ways to enjoy different arrangements.

## point

### 1

## Any kind of glass container is OK

Creating vegetation inside a transparent glass container—this is the most basic thing in regard to terrariums. This book includes many of the different kinds of containers for terrariums on the market. However, it doesn't have to be a container specifically for terrariums, and various kinds of glass containers can be used. For example, we can use flower vases for cut flowers, a display case with a wooden frame, or even more familiar items such as lampshades or bottles or pots from the kitchen. According to the specific characteristics of the plants, containers either have their lids closed, or left open for a change of air.

## point

### 2

## Showing the layers of soil from the side

The soil and material used in the base not only function as mix for growing the plants but are an important element of the terrarium to be enjoyed for their color and texture. Keeping in mind the view from the side of the container, take care to create beautiful layers including soil and chips, whitish sand and green moss. The kind of container used will also change according to where it will be placed. If placing on the floor or in low places, choose something large that will look pretty from above. When placed on a shelf or beside a wall, the terrarium will be viewed from the side so thinner containers or those that are taller are OK. When displaying in the kitchen, or where they are surrounded by many other objects, a slim and simple shape is better.

# Balance out the positioning of plants in the terrarium and make it attractive to look from any angle

As well the view from the side and from above, terrariums can also be viewed from below, with hanging types. When creating the terrarium, keep in mind which angle it will mainly be viewed from, and arrange it so that it looks good from any angle, not just one aspect. To do that, instead of arranging various plants and material in a straight line, position them so that they are to the front or behind the center, or to the left or right. This will give the composition more depth. Do not make a central piece in the container but place the main elements off to the side to create a feeling of imbalance. This will give a better result. Turn the container around as you are making the terrarium and check it out from different angles.

Aqua soil used for planting orchids

Wet cryptomeria bark used as a base for planting moss

# Improvise with the soil mix to ensure good drainage

As terrariums use glass containers with no hole in the bottom, water will not drain out of the container. It is important to choose soil mix that will facilitate good drainage while still retaining some moisture, so that water does not accumulate in the bottom of the container. Use a soil mix a large ratio of rice husk charcoal mixed in, which will help to control unwanted bacteria, or use aqua soil which is quite effective at retaining moisture. Sometimes plants are planted directly in bark chips, popular as a mulching material. The sand layer not only makes the terrarium look more attractive but also has good drainage and aeration qualities, appropriate for terrariums. Using different soil conditioners is good as it enables various beneficial results. Also, do not forget to always use material to prevent root rot in the bottom of the container.

Various kinds of soil are mixed together with Akadama soil, or red ball soil, as the base. The distinguishing feature of soil for terrariums is the large ratio of rice husk charcoal that is mixed in.

## Incorporating natural materials

1. Driftwood: Pieces with many small branches, or that are curved, those with complex shapes are recommended.
2. Banana stems: Banana stems that have been dried. Accentuate their long extended line.
3. Cauliflower roots: Cauliflower roots that have been dried.
4. Dried fungi: Arrange them with an image of how they would look growing in a forest.
5. Cork: A naturally occurring material from the bark of cork oak trees.
6. Driftwood: Sometimes used as a base due to excellent drainage qualities.
7. Coconut husk: Roots can be attached to pieces of coconut husk.

*point*

# 5

# Recreating a natural growth area with various materials

The unique appeal of terrariums lies in using various materials such as stones, driftwood and branches, as well as soil, and enjoying their textures and combinations. This is made possible because compared to ordinary planting, watering is more infrequent. Almost anything could be used but in order to create a natural atmosphere, it is better to choose material keeping in mind the environment in which plants would be growing naturally. For example, for cactus that grows in a dry environment, try using sand as the base complemented by coral, cork or others. For air plants, affixing them to stones with crevices gives the appearance that they grow there naturally. Incorporating banana stems or branches that evoke movement, materials that have a strong presence themselves, can be fun.

Pieces of branches from a mulberry tree are used as an accent amongst plants.

A piece of cork made to look like a rock, placed among a group of small cacti.

# Enjoying various combinations of plants

A miniature world of nature can be created behind the glass of a terrarium by planting various kinds of plants together. Care needs to be taken to combine plants that grow in the same kind of habitat. For moss, if you use the same kind of plants that grow in places where the moss grows naturally, they are sure to be well matched. Ferns are the kind of plant that likes high humidity, making them ideal for terrariums. Planting together succulents with different colors, shapes, and textures will give a rich and vibrant impression. First of all you can enjoy simple combinations of just one kind of plant and material but as you get used to creating terrariums, why don't you try group plantings.

Observing plants growing in places near you may offer hints for combination planting.

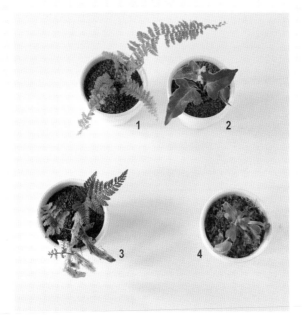

## Plants well suited to moss

Plants typically suited to planting with moss include ferns, which like a very humid environment, and insectivorous plants. The moisture retaining ability of moss keeps the inside of the terrarium at an appropriate degree of humidity.

1. *Nephrolepis*: A genus of fern with coarsely toothed leaves and used as an ornamental plant.
2. *Pyrrosia lingua*: A fern with simple undivided leaves.
3. *Davallia mariesii*: A fern native to Japan.
4. *Dionaea muscipula*: An insectivorous plant the same as *Nepenthes*.

# Choose a container that matches the plants' rate of growth

After the terrarium has been made, it may become cramped as the plants grow. Choose a container with some leeway to allow for the expected growth of the plants in it. If they are the kind of plants that grow tall, then choose a container with some height and leave the upper part free to allow for growth. If the plants are the kind that grows horizontally, choose a shallow round container. Plants that are slow growers, like cacti, can be planted in a container just the right size as they are unlikely to outgrow it. However, taking into consideration the layers of soil and material to be used, the terrarium will look better if a container that seems even a little too big than needed is used.

# Take care not to get the glass dirty

An important point with terrariums is to keep the glass clean and looking beautiful. When putting materials in the terrarium, take care not to dirty the glass. When adding soil to the container, use a funnel or tool with a small mouth to put the soil inside neatly and so that it won't fall on top of the plants already inside. When putting plants in a container that is long sideways, sit them on a ruler and slide them in gently. Finally, check that there is no soil on the inside of the glass or on the plants and give a final finishing off with a brush. If the spray is too strong when you water the plants, soil may get splattered around so be careful.

## Necessary Tools

When making a terrarium in a container that is difficult to reach inside,
it is very convenient to have a range of tools to help with awkward tasks.

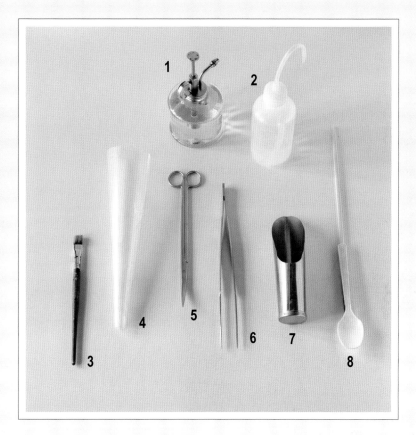

1. Spray: Moss and air plants are watered with a spray so you need to have a spray.
2. A watering bottle with a nozzle: Convenient when watering a terrarium with a narrow neck,
   or to avoid getting water on the leaves of certain plants.
3. Brush: To brush soil off leaves or the sides of the container, or to brush the surface of the soil.
4. Funnel: This one is made from a clear plastic folder. Used when putting soil or sand in a container,
   so it doesn't scatter around.
5. Scissors: Long scissors sold for using in aquariums.
6. Tweezers: Necessary for planting plants. Easier to use than long chopsticks used in cooking.
7. Metal scoop: For spreading soil or sand in a small space.
8. Spoon: To use instead of a scoop. This spoon has been attached to a long chopstick for extra length.

# Types of Soil

As well as choosing the right soil for the plants in the terrarium,
various kinds of soil may be used in just one terrarium,
to make layers and as the final decorative layer on top.

### ① Vermiculite

Vermiculite is a sterile soil made from a mineral fired to a high temperature. The nooks and crannies on its surface and its lightness are the distinguishing features of vermiculite. It is permeable and also has water retention qualities. It is better mixed with peat moss or Akadama soil.

### ② Aqua soil

Good quality dark soil has been fired to make it granular. As a substrate material for growing aquatic plants, it maintains water quality. Aqua soil has good aeration qualities and is suited to moss and so on, in terrariums.

### ③ Bark chips

Often used as a mulching material for the surface of soil. Due to its excellent aeration qualities, it is spread directly in terrariums that do not use soil.

### ④ Akadama soil

A basic type of soil used generally in horticulture. It is granular in texture and made from red soil from the Kanto loam. It is permeable and also has good water retention qualities. It is used in this book as a base for soil mix.

### ⑤ Peat moss

Sphagnum moss and other plant material that have compacted in layers over time. It has excellent permeability and water retention qualities. As it is lightweight, it is often sued in hanging baskets and terrariums. The peat moss used in this book has had the PH altered.

### ⑥ Sphagnum moss

A kind of moss that grows in marshy land. The balance of its permeability and water retention qualities is good and is known as a good material for planting orchids. When creating terrariums, sphagnum moss is an essential material that is wrapped around plants' roots to protect them.

### ⑦ Soil mix

This soil mix is a blend of four parts Akadama soil: two parts rice husk charcoal: one part vermiculite: one part sand: and one part peat moss. To improve drainage, using a slightly higher ratio of rice husk charcoal is an important point.

### ⑧ Sand

River sand is used as a whitish colored sand for aquariums. Its excellent permeability and water retention qualities make it suitable for terrariums too. It is used to make layers with soil and moss and also sandy landscapes can be recreated.

### ⑨ Cryptomeria bark

It has excellent water retention qualities. In the natural world many kinds of moss like to grown on tree bark or leaf mold so cryptomeria bark is suited to using with moss in terrariums.

### ⑩ Rice husk charcoal

Rice husk is smoked until it becomes charcoal. As it is good for adjusting humidity and preventing root rot, it is used in a higher ratio in soil for terrariums compared to for ordinary horticulture.

### ⑪ Ceramic

Granular ceramic with porous qualities. Can be used the same as soil for growing plants in planters or in aquaculture. Its distinguishing features are good permeability and water retention, and is often used for growing plants in containers without drainage holes.

### ⑫ Kanuma soil

A kind of pumice stone mainly produced in Kanuma city in Tochigi prefecture. The grains are compact and do not break down easily, enabling it to keep its permeability and water retention qualities for a long time. In this book, Kanuma soil is used in the blended soil mix.

# Characteristics of Each Plant and How to Look After Them

If you know the characteristics of the plants and can create
a nurturing environment for them inside the terrarium,
you will able to enjoy them for a long time.

## Succulents

## Combining plants from the same group is the key: Either winter dormant or summer dormant

As succulents are able to store water in their thick leaves, stems and roots, their distinguishing feature is that they do not need frequent watering. They can be divided into three kinds of growth patterns: the spring/autumn type that grow in spring and autumn; the summer type that grows from early summer through to autumn; and the winter type that grows in winter. In the summer and winter types, some succulents are quite extreme. The winter type doesn't like hot weather and needs extra care so when planting in groups, combining succulents from the same winter type make it easier to look after them. When planting, allow space in the terrarium for their future growth too.

**Growth patterns**

Summer types: *Euphorbia*, *Aloe*, *Kalanchoe*, *Graptolite*, *Sedum*
Winter types: *Lithops*, *Sempervivum*, *Conophytum*
Spring/Autumn types: *Senecio*, *Echeveria*, *Haworthia*

### A bright place indoors.
### Change the place according to the seasons

Fundamentally, terrariums should be placed indoors in a spot that is well ventilated and light and bright. Direct sunlight should be avoided but if kept where the plants don't get any sunlight at all, they will grow tall and straggly and the color of leaves won't be good. In winter, the space they are placed in should have some sun coming in. Succulents that don't like hot weather should be placed in semi-shade in summer.

Where to display

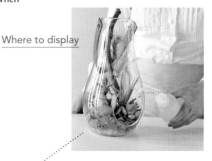

### Take care not to over-water

Water the plants using a container with a nozzle so that you can apply water directly to the roots and avoid getting water on the leaves. Terrariums require even less frequent watering than pot plants so do be careful not to over-water them. In growth phases, water once every four or five days. In dormant periods, water in a cycle of about every two weeks.

Watering

### Taking a plant out if necessary

Each plant grows at a different rate and you can usually grow them for about two years in a terrarium. When it gets to be too crowded overall, a way to resolve this is by taking out one plant. When removing the plant, press down on the roots of the other plants and with tweezers, pull out the plant you want to remove. Rather than trying to rearrange it, leave the other plants to fill the space naturally.

Replanting

### Prune leaves if they get too long

Plants that have definitely had it should be pulled out instead of trying to prune them. However, for leaves that are too long, simply pinching (pruning) the ends is all that is needed. Maintenance is very easy.

Maintenance

---------- Air Plants ----------

# Choose a well ventilated place. Be sure to dry properly after watering

Air plants are another name for plants belonging to the *Tillandias* genus of the Ananas family. They came to be called this as it looks like they grow in air in their natural rocky environment. They absorb moisture from the air so do not need frequent watering. However, if they are not watered at all, they will die just like other plants. After being placed in a terrarium, air plants need periodic watering and it is important to completely dry them off before returning them to the terrarium.

### Be careful of direct sunlight on the glass

Display in a bright place indoors. The same as succulents, air plants will not grow where they do not get any sunlight. However, direct sunlight must be avoided. This is because direct sunlight hitting a terrarium will make the temperature inside rise thus creating a steam bath. Good ventilation is also important. However, the air flow from air conditioning hitting a plant will dry it out too much, so take care to avoid this.

### After watering with a spray, completely drying it out is the trick

Once or twice a week, take the plant out of its container and spray the ends of the leaves. With good ventilation, dry it completely before returning to its container. If there is water around the roots, turn the plant upside down and shake it. Soaking in water is another way to water plants but as moisture may collect around the roots, this method is not recommended. Plants with green leaves seem to want water more than those with silver leaves.

### If the plant increases in size, switch to a larger container

As air plants are not planted in soil, they don't need replanting. If the leaves have increased in size, change them over to a terrarium that is larger.

### Remove leaves that have turned brown

The distinguishing feature of air plants is that they do not need much maintenance. However, any leaves that have gone brown will attract bugs so remove any such leaves when you find them. Use the tweezers to gently pull off the outside leaves.

Where to display

Watering

Replanting

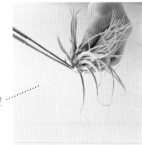

Maintenance

## Moss

# As long as the environment is compatible, mosses can be freely combined with other plants

Japan's climate suits mosses and many different kinds grow here. Not having roots, moss can be peeled off where they are growing and simply placed on the top layer of soil in a terrarium, and they will get used to that environment. They can grow in airtight spaces too, making it possible to choose from a wide range of containers. Moss has an image of only growing in the shade but some mosses like partial shade so it pays to refer to their native environment. They are especially easy to grow with ferns which like the same kind of damp environment.

### Growth patterns

Full shade: *Pyrrhobryum dozyanum, Bartramia pomiformis, Dicranales, Fissidens, Bazzania pompeana, Thuidium*
Partial shade: *Leucobryum juniperoideum, Entodon rubicundus, Plagiomnium acutum, Leucobryum bowringii Mitt.*

Where to display

### Good for putting in places where there is not a lot of sunlight

Depending on where they grow naturally, mosses prefer either shade (not completely dark but slightly dark), or partial shade (no direct sunlight but with some sunlight shining through such as on a forest floor). They should be placed in either of these places, according to what suits them.

### Maintain humidity by spraying with water, if it seems dry

When freshly planted, moss should be watered very well to enable it to become attached to the soil below it. Usually moss should be watered when the surface appears dry. Spray from the mouth of the container. That may change depending on what is planted together with the moss, where the terrarium is placed, and whether or not it has a lid. Roughly speaking, it should be watered once every three or four days.

Watering

### Take out one bunch of moss while pressing down on the other plants in the terrarium

Moss doesn't grow all that quickly so it should not need to be replanted very frequently. But if there is some moss that seems overgrown, pull it out while pressing down on the other plants so they don't come out too. The same as with succulents, the new space should fill in naturally without having to move other plants in the terrarium.

Replanting

### Cut out any moss that has changed color

If moss has turned yellow or brown from getting overgrown, you can cut out the places that have changed color. The moss will put forth new growth in that spot. You can grow more moss by cutting off a part that has grown considerably, and propagate it by planting it somewhere else.

Maintenance

# Orchids

## Orchids grow in various places. The planting style depends on whether the orchid is a terrestrial or epiphyte

It has been said that in the plant world, orchids were late to evolve. Because of that, they have developed ways to survive in various environments such as places without much sunlight, or by attaching themselves to trees. Growth patterns are divided into two types: terrestrials which grow on the ground: and epiphytes which grow by attaching their roots to trees or rocks, etc. The flowers are very attractive. However, arranging the plant so that the thick leaves or bulbous roots (the part where stems have become round and fleshy) can be viewed brings out the true appeal of terrariums.

### Growth patterns

Epiphytes: *Midi Phalaenopsis, Oncidium, Dendrobium*
Terrestrials: *Paphiopedilum, Cymbidium*

### Types

Sympodial (puts out a new bulb every year from which multiple stems appear): *Oncidium, Dendrobium*
Monopodial (grows one central vertical stem): *Vanda, Midi Phalaenopsis*

### Orchids can be displayed in the front entrance area and other places, without having to worry too much about direct sun

Plants will get scorched by direct sunlight so partial shade is ideal. In the house, orchids can be displayed in areas like the front entrance that don't get a lot of sun, as well as near windows in the living room. Orchids will be stressed until they get used to the new environment but they are capable of adapting.

Where to display

Watering

### Water with the same frequency, even if the way they are planted is different

Surprisingly enough, orchids are good at retaining moisture so they only need watering with a spray when they get dry. Terrestrial types can be watered from the mouth of the container. Epiphytes should be taken out of the container together with their wood base and mainly the roots sprayed with water. The same as with other plants, orchids must be properly dried before being returned to their container. It is not good for their roots to always be wet.

Epiphytes can be taken out and maintenance done by pinching off leaves. However, tools for the terrarium such as tweezers and scissors are very handy to use.

### Remove leaves that are no good anymore

Remove any stems or leaves that have died or changed color. Only remove that part. Plants that have become too big are difficult to maintain so those in pots need to be divided up. One of those smaller plants can be attached to some cork. The more compact the plant is, the easier maintenance is.

Maintenance

# Troubleshooting Terrariums

Growing plants in terrariums is somewhat different to growing them in pots. Here are some of the issues that people face when creating a terrarium for the first time.

## Q. The moss has changed to a brownish color.

— A —

Moss that has turned brown will never go back to being green again. But don't worry; it doesn't mean that all the moss is no good. If you cut out all the moss that has gone brown, new green moss will grow back in its place.

## Q. What pests should I be careful about?

— A —

Be careful of pests such as tiny aphids (sticky when touched) that appear when the terrarium heats up; black spot disease which causes brown or black spots on plants; and in summer, be on the lookout for mites. If there are not too many, you can remove the pests with tweezers and then use some kind of insecticide. If there are quite a lot, remove the plants and check the roots. If the roots are black, it means the plants have had it.

## Q. The succulent leaves have become dried out.

## Q. I've watered my terrarium too much and now water has accumulated in the bottom of the container.

## Q. Can I give my terrarium some fertilizer? When should I do it?

— A —

Terrariums don't really need fertilizer but if you want to, you could dilute liquid fertilizer at a ratio of one part liquid fertilizer to 2,000 parts water. Regarding timing, give the fertilizer during the growth periods of each plant. Air plants, which are not planted in soil, can be sprayed with water that has a small amount of liquid fertilizer mixed into it. However, moss does not require any fertilizer at all.

— A —

It depends on the type of succulent, but if they are just a bit shriveled up, they may recover. If the leaves of *Haworthia* are hard and dry, and turned red, then that means they have completely had it. Remove these leaves by pulling them off. If it is a succulent with various branches and only one branch has changed color at the tip, then cut that part off.

— A —

Water cannot be drained from a terrarium as there is no hole in the bottom of the container. So to remove the water, it has to be absorbed with a tissue. Use tweezers to tap the rolled up tissue on to the surface of the soil. It takes a little time and effort but this way, the tissue will absorb the excess water.

## 1 *Astroloba bullulata*

Asphodelaceae Family, *Astroloba* Genus

This plant's shape is similar to those of the Haworthia family with hard, dense leaves. The triangular pyramid-shaped compact leaves form a star shape, and grow upwards, one on top of another, densely covering the stems, like a tower. The leaves are a deep green color and smooth, with some plants have pale inconspicuous spots.

● Growth pattern: Spring/Autumn type
● Approximate size: Around 4in/10cm tall

## 2 *Pachyphytum* cv. Gekkabijin

Crassulaceae Family, *Pachyphytum* Genus

The pastel-colored, rounded, plump and fleshy leaves are very cute. The surface of the leaves has a powdery white coating while the outer edges are pinkish. In autumn, it turns a reddish color. In spring, it bears flowers. As it stores water in its thick leaves, it does not need frequent watering. Can be propagated by dividing plants or by leaf cuttings.

● Growth pattern: Summer type
● Approximate size: A diameter of 4in/10cm

## 3 *Senecio stapeliiformis*

Asteraceae Family, *Senecio* Genus

Erect and long stems that are hard and like rods. The surface is covered with leaves like small thorns that are spaced at regular intervals. It has fleshy strong roots and the stems increase as the plant grows. A bright orange flower blooms in spring providing a unique contrast with the thick stems.

● Growth pattern: Spring/Autumn type
● Approximate size: Around 10in/25cm tall

## 4 *Graptopetalum* cv. Snow White

Crassulaceae Family, *Graptopetalum* Genus

Also known by names such as Hime-ob-orozuki or Ginkoren in Japan. Its large rosettes, typical of *Graptopetalums*, and pale greenish coloring are quite attractive. Do not water much in summer and winter. Basically it should be kept in a fairly dry state. Avoid direct sunlight and place in partial shade so the leaves don't get burnt.

● Growth pattern: Spring/Autumn type
● Approximate size: A diameter of 2–4in /5–10cm

## 5 *Rhipsalis pilocarpa*

Cactaceae Family, *Rhipsalis* Genus

One of a group of approximately 60 kinds of cacti that grow on trees in subtropical or tropical rainforests. The typical shape is a thin ropelike stem growing quite tall and often hanging over the side of the pot. Good for planting in a hanging container indoors.

● Growth pattern: Spring/Autumn type
● Approximate size: 20–24in/50–60cm tall

## 6 *Sedum* cv. Alice Evans

Crassulaceae Family, Sedum Genus

The fresh green thick leaves form tight rosettes. These plump leaves store water making the plant resistant to dry and cold conditions. Able to tolerate winter outside, apart from cold areas. If the stem grows long, cut it and push into soil to propagate.

● Growth pattern: Spring/Autumn type
● Approximate size: A diameter of 3–4in /8–10cm

### 1  *Crassula* cv. Blue Bird

Crassulaceae Family, *Crassula* Genus

Belonging to the same group as *Crassula ovata*, (aka money tree), the leaves of *Crassula* cv. Blue Bird are a strong blue-green color. The round, thick, flattish leaves are covered in a blue-white powder while having a red edge to them. The plant is strong with a trunk and if able to survive for a few years, will take on a sturdy tree-like shape.

● Growth pattern: Summer type
● Approximate size: 40–120in/1–3m tall

### 2  *Pachyveria* cv. Blue Mist

Crassulaceae Family, *Pachyphytum* Genus

The leaves look like jelly beans as they are thick and roundish in shape. The delicate coloring of pale purple *Pachyveria* cv. Blue Mist covered in a white powder is beautiful and it shows out in a group planting. In summer keep it in bright shade and keep it fairly dry. It will not tolerant the cold well and needs to be put indoors in winter. Propagate by cuttings.

● Growth pattern: Spring/Autumn type
● Approximate size: A diameter of 2in/5cm

### 3  *Echeveria* cv. Pallida Prince

Crassulaceae Family, *Echeveria* Genus

A medium-sized *Echeveria*, also known as the Prime Minister of Flowers in Japanese. The pale green rosettes of leaves are very pretty. The red edging makes the leaves almost seem as though they are made of wax and is very attractive. Propagate by cuttings. Dormant in summer, it needs to be shielded from direct sunlight so its leaves won't get burnt. Needs to be looked after indoors in winter.

● Growth pattern: Spring/Autumn type
● Approximate size: A diameter of 8in/20cm

### 4  *Sempervivum* cv. Lipari

Crassulaceae Family, *Sempervivum* Genus

*Sempervivum* means "forever alive" in Latin. A middle class succulent, they are robust of nature and very tolerant of cold. The long narrow leaves that are blue-green in color are beautiful and change color with the seasons. Be careful not to overwater.

● Growth pattern: Winter type
● Approximate size: A diameter of 2–4in/5–10cm

### 5  *Orostachys genkaiense*

Crassulaceae Family, *Orostachys* Genus

The rosettes made up of round-shaped leaves of this succulent are very cute. It is a hardy plant good at reproducing itself. Mature plants put out runners to produce lots of baby plants. Flowers bloom in autumn with a thin stalk growing from the center of a rosette to form a white flower. They are very tolerant of the cold and it is possible to grow it outside even in mid-winter.

● Growth pattern: Spring/Autumn type
● Approximate size: 4in/10cm or shorter

### 6  *Graptopetalum paraguayense*

Crassulaceae Family, *Graptopetalum* Genus

This variety is often seen growing in profusion and hanging down off rock walls beside roads. The leaves which develop rosettes are a pale pink and covered in a white powder. They are extremely hardy and can be grown all year round outside. They only need watering twice a month, to the extent that the soil becomes wet, not a complete soaking.

● Growth pattern: Summer type
● Approximate size: 4–6in/10–15cm tall

### 1  *Astrophytum ornatum*

Cactaceae Family, *Astrophytum* Genus

This cactus has eight ridges and sharp brown spines. As it grows, the shape changes from round to columnar. Some may grow to be more than one meter tall. There are several varieties such as *Astrophytum ornatum* var. *mirbelii* or var. *glabrescens* which have different colors and patterns. Give this cactus lots of water during its growth period from spring through to autumn, but do not water in winter.

● <u>Growth pattern:</u> **Summer type**
● <u>Approximate size:</u> **4–8in/10–20cm tall**

### 4  *Notocactus scopa* var. *ruberrimus*

Cactaceae Family, *Notocactus* Genus

This beautiful, small, dome-shaped cactus is covered with white spines. In spring, buds that look like brown berries appear on the top of the cactus. After swelling up over a period of two days, a cluster of bright yellow flowers bloom simultaneously. It is hardy and resistant to cold but in extremely hot areas it should be sheltered from the sun and left to be semi-dormant.

● <u>Growth pattern:</u> **Summer type**
● <u>Approximate size:</u> **A diameter of 2–4in /5–10cm**

### 2  *Chamaecereus silvestrii*

Cactaceae Family, *Chamaecereus* Genus

This is a clumping columnar cactus with stems of a diameter of 0.8–1.2in/2–3cm which grow like rope, lying on the surface of the soil until they overflow from the edge of the pot. It produces numerous scarlet flowers from late spring to early summer. Can be grown outdoors. It likes plenty of sun and good ventilation. Do not water in winter.

● <u>Growth pattern:</u> **Summer type**
● <u>Approximate size:</u> **8–12in/20–30cm tall**

### 5  *Pseudolithos migiurtinus*

Apocynaceae Family, *Pseudolithos* Genus

This ball-shaped cactus originates from Somalia. The genus name *Pseudolithos* means "false stone" and refers to their round shape and unique pebble-like appearance. Small brown flowers emerge from the cactus stem. Very tolerant of direct sun in midsummer and can be grown outdoors.

● <u>Growth pattern:</u> **Summer type**
● <u>Approximate size:</u> **A diameter of 2in/5cm**

### 3  *Echinocereus rigidissimus* subsp. *rubispinus*

Cactaceae Family, *Echinocereus* Genus

A subspecies of *Echinocereus rigidissimus*, this cactus grows in a columnar shape, becoming larger towards the top. Its purplish/pink gradation is colorful and the reddish/magenta radial spines are neatly arranged. In spring, pink flowers bloom on the top of the plant. No watering in winter, and plenty of sun will improve the coloring of the flowers and the cactus itself.

● <u>Growth pattern:</u> **Summer type**
● <u>Approximate size:</u> **6–12in/15–30cm tall**

1      2      3      4      5

## 1 *Dorstenia hildebrandtii* f. *crispum*

Moraceae Family, *Dorstenia* Genus

*Dorstenia* have a somewhat different form to what we are used to, comprising what are called "leaf succulents." The leaves are thin and wavy while the base of the stem is bulbous. This succulent grows from seedlings. The seeds are propelled a long way from the parent plant. It does not tolerate cold well and needs to be grown inside in winter.

● <u>Growth pattern:</u> Summer type
● <u>Approximate size:</u> 4–6in/10–15cm tall

## 4 *Crassula lycopodioides* var. *pseudolycopodioides*

Crassulaceae Family, *Crassula* Genus

The light green slender leaves growing ropelike in a cluster are this plant's main feature. The leaves can grow as high as 12in/30cm but cutting them back to about 4in/10cm makes them look neater. In autumn, tiny yellow flowers peek out from among the leaves.

● <u>Growth pattern:</u> Spring/Autumn type
● <u>Approximate size:</u> 4–12in/10–30cm tall

## 2 *Huernia*

Apocynaceae Family, *Huernia* Genus

The bumpy ridges on the stems of this columnar succulent are its distinguishing feature. Well-known species include *Huernia brevirostris*, *Huernia thuretii* var. *primulina*, and *Huernia pillansii*. It does not have leaves and star-shaped flowers bloom directly on the stem. Some varieties have a smell typical of this genus. Avoid strong sun and grow in a well ventilated environment.

● <u>Growth pattern:</u> Summer type
● <u>Approximate size:</u> 8–12in/20–30cm tall

## 5 *Euphorbia mammillaris*

Euphorbiaceae Family, *Euphorbia* Genus

This plant looks similar to a cactus with its silver-colored stem and sharp spines. Apart from watering during its growth period, it does not need any special care. Produces small peach-colored flowers after achieved a certain amount of growth. Be careful of the poisonous white sap from the stems and leaves.

● <u>Growth pattern:</u> Spring/Autumn type
● <u>Approximate size:</u> 12in/30cm tall

## 3 *Tephrocactus articulates* f. *diadematus*

Cactaceae Family, *Tephrocactus* Genus

A species of cactus in the same subfamily as prickly pear cacti, it grows in globular to elongated stem segments. The flattened spines which appear from stem joints are like paper, making this plant easy to remember. Segments of the round stems may fall off after they have grown to a certain degree. These can be propagated by pushing into soil.

● <u>Growth pattern:</u> Spring/Autumn type
● <u>Approximate size:</u> 8in/20cm tall

### 1 *Sulcorebutia rauschii*

Cactaceae Family, *Sulcorebutia* Genus

The Japanese name is Kokureimaru. This small, plump globular cactus produces new growth with clumps of many heads packed together. Color variations of the cacti epidermis exist including purple and green. In early spring, beautiful pink flowers appear. The root can become quite big so replant it at an opportune time.

● Growth pattern: Spring/Autumn type
● Approximate size: A diameter of 1.2–2in /3–5cm

### 2 *Frailea*

Cactaceae Family, *Frailea* Genus

Many plants in the *Frailea* genus have cute names in Japanese such as, Baby Tiger, Baby Racoon Dog, and Baby Leopard. This is a very small globular cactus, but even at a size of about 2cm, it bears yellow flowers. It needs quite a lot of water during its growth period and should be grown in soft light, shielded from direct sunlight.

● Growth pattern: Summer type
● Approximate size: A diameter of 1.2–2in /3–5cm

### 3 *Sempervivum arachnoideum*

Crassulaceae Family, *Sempervivum* Genus

As its name implies, the rosettes have white fur on their tips like cobwebs. It is resistant to cold and easy to grow. After replanting in spring, a cluster of pups will appear. As the roots are quite fine, it is better to replant it before it grows too big.

● Growth pattern: Winter type
● Approximate size: A diameter of 1.2in/3cm

### 4 *Ophthalmophyllum*

Aizoaceae Family, *Lithops* Genus

One of a group of plants called *Messembryanthemum* where the leaves have become round and fleshy. The group includes diverse varieties such as *Ophthalmophyllum friedrichiae*. The top of the leaf is split into two and many of these plants are translucent. It is active in winter and completely dormant in summer, when it should be managed by not watering.

● Growth pattern: Winter type
● Approximate size: 0.8–1.2in/2–3cm tall

### 5 *Haworthia truncata*

Asphodelaceae Family, *Haworthia* Genus

The thick leaves fan out and arranged in vertical rows. The upper part seems almost to have been cut with a knife. The tip of the leaf is translucent allowing light to enter for photosynthesis. This plant has thick and long roots so it is better to grow it in a pot for orchids.

● Growth pattern: Spring/Autumn type
● Approximate size: A diameter of 2in/5cm

### 6 *Lithops julii* subsp. *fulleri*

Aizoaceae Family, *Lithops* Genus

Some types have different colors such as red or brown. This plant has a translucent window on the crown and markings like cracks. In spring and autumn, it sheds its skin from the crack in the middle and starts to clump by putting forth new leaves. After shedding skin, the leaves become wrinkly but do not give in to the temptation to give them extra water.

● Growth pattern: Winter type
● Approximate size: 1.2–2in/3–5cm tall

### 1  *Rhipsalis cassutha*

Cactaceae Family, *Rhipsalis* Genus

This is a typical variety of *Rhipsalis* with its slender stems growing every direction as they grow longer and longer. If the plant grows well, stems may reach a length of several meters. The same as for most cacti, do not water too much. Not tolerant of cold so try to keep the temperature indoors at 10°C or higher.

● **Growth pattern: Spring/Autumn type**
● **Approximate size: 20–24in/50–60cm long**

### 4  *Cereus spegazzinii* f. *cristatus*

Cactaceae Family, *Cereus* Genus

This columnar cactus is a mutant variety. The Japanese name is Zansetsu, which means "lingering snow." The parts of the cacti that seem to have become petrified and spread out like peaks of mountains appear to be covered with snow, which is the white fluff around the base of the spines. So it is quite an elegant name for this plant. Give it plenty of sun and if the bottom of the pot seems dry, give it plenty of water.

● **Growth pattern: Spring/Autumn type**
● **Approximate size: 8in/20cm tall**

### 2  *Echeveria cante*

Crassulaceae Family, *Echeveria* Genus

Known in Japan as the "Queen of *Echeveria*," *Echeveria cante* can form rosettes up to 30cm if the plant grows long enough, making it worthy of the title of queen. The pale green leaves, which layer one upon another, are covered with a white powder, while the edges of the leaves are pale pink. From autumn through winter, the color becomes more reddish.

● **Growth pattern: Spring/Autumn type**
● **Approximate size: A diameter of 8–12in /20–30cm**

### 5  *Argenteo*

Crassulaceae Family, *Sedum* Genus

In this type, the stems grow long and then hang down. It grows very well and any stems that come in contact with soil will sprout roots. Tolerant of heat and cold. The gradation of coloring of the leaves from silver to pink is charming. As it belongs to the *Sedum* genus, it needs more water than normal succulents.

● **Growth pattern: Spring/Autumn type**
● **Approximate size: 20in/50cm tall**

### 3  *Haworthia cooperi* var. *pilifera variegata*

Asphodelaceae Family, *Haworthia* Genus

One of the soft green group of *Haworthia*, the leaves have transparent windows similar to frosted glass. The root stock is hardy and when grown in clumps it looks very fresh and beautiful. It does not have spines and is a small plant making it easy to grow on a window sill or verandah. In summer it should be shielded from direct sunlight to prevent sunburn.

● **Growth pattern: Spring/Autumn type**
● **Approximate size: A diameter of 4in/10cm**

### 6  *Cissus cactiformis*

Vitaceae Family, *Cissus* Genus

The square columnar stems are noded. The stems have leaves with tendrils like feelers that wrap around them. The stems are a beautiful jade green, giving rise to the plants name in Japanese, Hisuikaku. However, despite their thickness, the stems break off easily. The fruit looks like grapes and they turn a reddish/purple color upon maturing. However, they are poisonous and cannot be eaten.

● **Growth pattern: Summer type**
● **Approximate size: 20–24in/50–60cm tall**

## 1 *Haworthia turgida*

Asphodelaceae Family, *Haworthia* Genus

A popular plant of the soft leaf *Haworthia* type. The tips of the thick triangular leaves have a transparent window and light showing through the stripes or spotted pattern creates a cool effect. Turns red under direct sunlight and may melt away, so shield from direct sunlight and place it in a bright environment.

● Growth pattern: Spring/Autumn type
● Approximate size: A diameter of 2–4in
/5–10cm

## 4 *Sempervivum* cv. Red Chief

Crassulaceae Family, *Sempervivum* Genus

The compact leaves rise up in a spiral to form a beautiful rosette. The leaves which change color with the seasons are appealing and it is especially attractive and quite impressive when it turns red in winter. The leaves have some fluff on the surface and it is tolerant of the cold, making it possible to grow outside even in winter.

● Growth pattern: Winter type
● Approximate size: A diameter of 2–4in
/5–10cm

## 2 *Haworthia* cv. Yumedono

Asphodelaceae Family, *Haworthia* Genus

There are many hybrids in the group of soft leaf *Haworthia* and this is one of them. The thick triangular leaves have the distinguishing feature windows for letting the light in. There are also tubercles, like white spines, all over the leaves. Its growth rate is rather slow but small plants will form at the leaf base so be patient in growing it.

● Growth pattern: Spring/Autumn type
● Approximate size: A diameter of 2–4in
/5–10cm

## 5 *Haworthia cooperi*

Asphodelaceae Family, *Haworthia* Genus

A member of the soft leaf *Haworthia* group which have a transparent window at the tip of the thick leaves, *Haworthia cooperi* has narrower leaves than similar plants in its group. New plants are freely produced at the base and when it clumps, it looks even prettier. It is easy to grow year round indoors with partial shade.

● Growth pattern: Winter type
● Approximate size: A diameter of 2–4in
/5–10cm

## 3 *Crassula mesembryanthemoides*

Crassulaceae Family, *Crassula* Genus

This plant is a subspecies of the very popular *Crassula* cv. Ginzoroe. The distinguishing feature of this plant is that the leaves are covered with soft bristle-like hairs. Compared to Ginzoroe the leaves are flatter and more long and narrow. It can be propagated by leaf cuttings. It is tolerant of the cold and dry conditions but does not like dampness. Be careful not to let it get wet in the rain.

● Growth pattern: Summer type
● Approximate size: 4–6in/10–15cm tall

### 1 *Kalanchoe pumila*

Crassulaceae Family, *Kalanchoe* Genus

The silver-green leaves, which look as though they have been dusted with powder, are beautiful. Their distinguishing feature is the toothed margins. Blooming over a long period from January to May, this plant bears clusters of pale pink flowers. Coupled with the silver leaves, this color combination is quite elegant. To maintain the color of the leaves, be careful of too much humidity.

● <u>Growth pattern</u>: **Summer type**
● <u>Approximate size</u>: **8in/20cm tall**

### 4 *Echeveria* cv. Rezry

Crassulaceae Family, *Echeveria* Genus

The leaves are thick and slightly elongated in shape, forming rosettes as they grow. The deep green leaves change to red when the temperature is low and in mid-winter, they turn a magenta color similar to bronze. It grows fairly quickly and the thick stems grow upwards, bending over as they do. The plant's shape is full of movement making it ideal for interior decor.

● <u>Growth pattern</u>: **Spring/Autumn type**
● <u>Approximate size</u>: **A diameter of 2–4in /5–10cm**

### 2 *Sedum rubens*

Crassulaceae Family, *Sedum* Genus

The plump leaves, which are shaped like beans, are very cute. After summer the leaves change from a fresh green color through to pale yellow, then orange, and finally a scarlet color in autumn. The leaves have a tendency to drop off easily but these can be propagated as leaf cuttings. Water twice a month, just enough to wet the soil.

● <u>Growth pattern</u>: **Spring/Autumn type**
● <u>Approximate size</u>: **4in/10cm tall**

### 5 *Echeveria shaviana*

Crassulaceae Family, *Echeveria* Genus

The leaves, which form large open rosettes, have wavy crinkled margins. As the number of leaves increases, the entire plant rises up, taking on an elegant appearance. In summer, remove the dead leaves that have fallen off at the base of the plant, to prevent the roots rotting and leaves changing color from dampness.

● <u>Growth pattern</u>: **Spring/Autumn type**
● <u>Approximate size</u>: **A diameter of 4–12in /10–30cm**

### 3 *Sedum* cv. Sunrise Mom

Crassulaceae Family, *Sedum* Genus

Also known as *Sedum* cv. Yellow Moon. The small thick leaves look like the moon when they are yellowish while they are reminiscent of sunrise when they change color in autumn to orange or red. The stems grow vertically. Propagated from leaves or cuttings, this *Sedum* is very small and cute making it extremely suitable for group plantings.

● <u>Growth pattern</u>: **Spring/Autumn type**
● <u>Approximate size</u>: **4–6in/10–15cm**

### 6 *Echeveria* cv. Shimo-no-ashita

Crassulaceae Family, *Echeveria* Genus

The thick leaves are of a pale bluish-white color. The tips are edged with pale pink, giving an accent to the overall paleness of the plant. Small salmon pink flowers bloom on a stalk that grows up robustly from the center of the plant. Grow in bright sunlight but be careful of high temperatures and humidity in mid-summer.

● <u>Growth pattern</u>: **Spring/Autumn type**
● <u>Approximate size</u>: **A diameter of 4–6in /10–15cm**

## 1  *Echeveria* cv. Takasago-no-okina

<u>Crassulaceae Family, *Echeveria* Genus</u>

This plant belongs to the group of *Echeveria* with leaves that have soft, wavy and frilly margins. The pale green leaves with pink edges turn a beautiful shade of red if they are grown with enough sunlight. It is a large variety and if the plant is healthy, it may grow to reach a diameter of 30cm or more. Having such a dynamic presence is what makes it appealing.

● <u>Growth pattern:</u> **Summer type**
● <u>Approximate size:</u> A diameter of 6–8in/15–20cm

## 4  *Kalanchoe rhombopilosa*

<u>Crassulaceae Family, *Kalanchoe* Genus</u>

Known in Japan by the names Senjaku or Himemiya, this plant's leaves are a blackish-brown or greenish-grey color with brown mottled markings. Both types have leaves that are frilly at the tips and wavy. The roots are quite fine and prone to root rot. The plant should be replanted when deemed appropriate.

● <u>Growth pattern:</u> **Summer type**
● <u>Approximate size:</u> 6–8in/15–20cm tall

## 2  *Adromischus cooperi*

<u>Crassulaceae Family, *Adromischus* Genus</u>

The *Adromischus* genus contains attractive succulents that have unique patterns or shapes. *Adromischus cooperi* has leaves which are rather flat and with wavy ends, and with a purple mottled pattern. Subspecies include paler and also tubular-shaped varieties. This plant does not like high temperatures and humidity. It is dormant in summer so do not water very often and leave it in a cool place.

● <u>Growth pattern:</u> **Spring/Autumn type**
● <u>Approximate size:</u> 4in/10cm tall

## 5  *Sempervivum* cv. Glaucum Mirror

<u>Crassulaceae Family, *Sempervivum* Genus</u>

The pointed flat leaves spread out radially to form beautiful rosettes. The center of the plant is a pale purple color, like a large flower. It is extremely cold resistant and can be grown outdoors even in mid-winter. It grows quickly and sends out lots of runners, so it should be replanted in spring.

● <u>Growth pattern:</u> **Winter type**
● <u>Approximate size:</u> A diameter of 2in/5cm

## 3  *Graptopetalum* cv. Bronze

<u>Crassulaceae Family, *Graptopetalum* Genus</u>

Shiny reddish-orange colored stems with thick triangular leaves that form small rosettes, rise up in clusters. The leaves have a tendency to come off easily but they can easily be propagated as leaf cuttings. Do not water much. If given lots of sun, the plant will change color to a reddish-bronze and become even more beautiful.

● <u>Growth pattern:</u> **Summer type**
● <u>Approximate size:</u> A diameter of 1.2in/3cm

## 6  *Sedum rubrotinctum*

<u>Crassulaceae Family, *Sedum* Genus</u>

The glossy plump leaves are quite cute. In summer they are a deep green but begin to turn red with the arrival of autumn. The gradation that occurs in that process is beautiful. By mid-autumn, the leaves and stems as well turn a bright red. The leaves can be used for leaf propagation or it can be used for decoration.

● <u>Growth pattern:</u> **Summer type**
● <u>Approximate size:</u> 4–6in/10–15cm tall

### 1  *Tillandsia juncifolia*

Bromeliaceae Family, *Tillandsia* Genus

This plant has long, slender, silver leaves that grow thickly, forming a shape like a broom. It has pretty reddish-purple flowers. It is quite similar to *Tillandsia juncea* but the trichome that covers *juncifolia* is thinner and of a darker blue color. Robust and with good propagating power, it is a plant that can be grown for quite a long time.

● <u>Growth pattern</u>: **Summer type**
● <u>Approximate size</u>: **6–8in/15–20cm tall**

### 2  *Tillandsia utriculata* clump

Bromeliaceae Family, *Tillandsia* Genus

Small type of the silver leaf variety. Its distinguishing feature is that it is reasonably quick to clump producing offsets or 'pups' even without flowering. Due to its simple shape, it is easy to observe the new offsets as they appear one after another. White flowers bloom on the red stems and after flowering, the parent plant dies.

● <u>Growth pattern</u>: **Summer type**
● <u>Approximate size</u>: **2–4in/5–10cm tall**

### 3  *Tillandsia pseudobaileyi*

Bromeliaceae Family, *Tillandsia* Genus

The name *pseudobaileyi* means a false bailey. It derives from the fact that there is already a plant called "baileyi" in this genus. The wavy tubular leaves of this plant are harder than the original variety. A large pot type, it requires a lot of water. If it gets too dry, the leaves become wrinkly. They revert to their true shape after watering.

● <u>Growth pattern</u>: **Summer type**
● <u>Approximate size</u>: **4–12in/10–30cm tall**

### 4  *Tillandsia funckiana*

Bromeliaceae Family, *Tillandsia* Genus

This is a small type of a caulescent, or stem-producing, plant with a slender soft stem that grows longer and longer. It clumps easily and depending on its environment, it may growing curly or in a round shape, giving an impression of movement. The scarlet flowers are surprisingly attractive. It like a bright environment with partial shade and is not very tolerant of cold.

● <u>Growth pattern</u>: **Summer type**
● <u>Approximate size</u>: **4–8in/10–20cm tall**

### 5  *Tillandsia streptophylla*

Bromeliaceae Family, *Tillandsia* Genus

A popular plant with a roundish shape. When the leaves become dehydrated, they curl up into tight ringlets. After absorbing water, the leaves straighten up again. It is fun to observe the changes in the plant depending on how much water it receives. Pale purple flowers form on pink inflorescences. It takes a few years until the plant matures enough to produce offsets.

● <u>Growth pattern</u>: **Summer type**
● <u>Approximate size</u>: **4–6in/10–15cm tall**

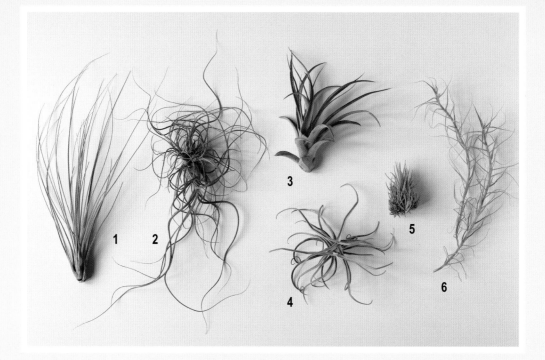

### 1  *Tillandsia juncea*

Bromeliaceae Family, *Tillandsia* Genus

This is a species that has silver needle-like leaves which grow to be quite long. Its slender form conveys a feeling of coolness and is well suited to displaying indoors. It is a robust plant and can tolerant dryness while it is comparatively resistant to heat and cold. Water by spraying with mist about three times weekly, and in spring and autumn water by soaking twice monthly.

● Growth pattern: **Spring/Autumn type**
● Approximate size: **6–8in/15–20cm tall**

### 2  *Tillandsia butzii* clump

Bromeliaceae Family, *Tillandsia* Genus

*Butzii* is recognizable because of its spotted wavy leaves that grow in all directions. It clumps easily and if left undivided, this will provide more volume, making quite an impressive display.

● Growth pattern: **Summer type**
● Approximate size: **8–10in/20–25cm tall**

### 3  *Tillandsia brachycaulos*

Bromeliaceae Family, *Tillandsia* Genus

This green leaf species has fleshy and somewhat hard leaves which change to a bright red color before and after flowering. Purple flowers bloom in the center of the plant and combined with the leaves which have turned bright red, it is very beautiful just like fireworks. It likes moisture and could be grow in in a pot on top of a layer of sphagnum moss.

● Growth pattern: **Spring/Autumn type**
● Approximate size: **4–6in/10–15cm tall**

### 4  *Tillandsia reichenbachii*

Bromeliaceae Family, *Tillandsia* Genus

The silvery-gray leaves are rather hard and wavy. *Reichenbachii* clumps easily. Pale purple flowers with a lovely fragrance bloom from June to July. Water by spraying with mist twice weekly.

● Growth pattern: **Summer type**
● Approximate size: **6–8in/15–20cm wide**

### 5  *Tillandsia loliacea*

Bromeliaceae Family, *Tillandsia* Genus

This *Tillandsia* is smaller than the size of your palm. From the center of the hard leaves covered with trichome, a long flower spike emerges with delicate yellow flowers about 3mm in size. It propagates easily, producing offsets frequently. This species is self-pollinating and flowers a few times throughout the year.

● Growth pattern: **Summer type**
● Approximate size: **About 1.2in/3cm tall**

### 6  *Tillandsia caerulea*

Bromeliaceae Family, *Tillandsia* Genus

The beautiful and slender silvery-green leaves appear one after another on the plant's stems, almost like branches on a tree. The scented purple flowers are very attractive. It likes a sunny and airy environment and will grow well hanging upside down from the roots.

● Growth pattern: **Summer type**
● Approximate size: **12–16in/30–40cm tall**

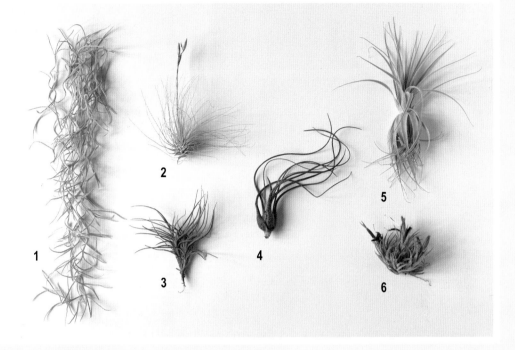

### 1 *Tillandsia usneoides*

Bromeliaceae Family, *Tillandsia* Genus

Also known as Spanish moss, the slender silver leaves intertwine with one another as the strands grow to be fluffy and long. Various species include a curly variety, large leaves, middle-sized leaves and so on. It has yellow scented flowers. Good for using as interior décor by draping over beams or on walls.

- **Growth pattern: Summer type**
- **Approximate size: 12–20in/30–50cm long**

### 2 *Tillandsia fuchsii*

Bromeliaceae Family, *Tillandsia* Genus

Silver leaves like wire grow in all four directions from the center of the clump. The flowers bloom on a long spike and the contrast between the red inflorscence and the purple petals of the flowers is wonderful. Produces offsets easily. Mist with a spray once every four or five days and grow in partial shade.

- **Growth pattern: Spring/Autumn type**
- **Approximate size: 2–4in/5–10cm tall**

### 3 *Tillandsia bandensis*

Bromeliaceae Family, *Tillandsia* Genus

This silver leaf species produces pale purple flowers with a lovely fragrance every year. It is a fan-shaped clustering plant. *Tillandsia mallemontii* is closely related but when the two are compared, the leaves of *bandensis* are somewhat harder. It is tolerant of cold and likes high moisture. However, be careful to grow it in an airy place as it doesn't like a hot and stuffy environment.

- **Growth pattern: Summer type**
- **Approximate size: 2in/5cm tall**

### 4 *Tillandsia butzii*

Bromeliaceae Family, *Tillandsia* Genus

The plant has a bulbous base while the long slender leaves curl upwards. The entire plant has a mottled pattern and is reminiscent of a snake. *Butzii* does not like summer heat and humidity so it needs to be grown in a cool place in summer. At the same time, it does not like to be dry so be generous with watering.

- **Growth pattern: Spring/Autumn type**
- **Approximate size: 4–6in/10–15cm tall**

### 5 *Tillandsia gardneri*

Bromeliaceae Family, *Tillandsia* Genus

This small variety of the *Tillandsia* genus is covered with trichome like rough fuzz and which reminds one of velour. The leaves spread out radially from the center and as they grow, they drape down and curl. It produces cute pink flowers. Mist so the plant does not dry out and grow by hanging.

- **Growth pattern: Summer type**
- **Approximate size: 8–12in/20–30cm tall**

### 6 *Tillandsia ionantha* clump

Bromeliaceae Family, *Tillandsia* Genus

*Ionantha* is one of the most popular species of the Tillandsia family. It is a prolific pupper and will form clumps easily. The real pleasure of growing *ionantha* is taking care of it until the clump grows in volume and forms a ball. The contrast between the silver, pink and purple colors in the period leading up to its bloom cycle is wonderful.

- **Growth pattern: Summer type**
- **Approximate size: 2–3in/5-8cm tall**

## 1  Tillandsia stricta

Bromeliaceae Family, *Tillandsia* Genus

*Tillandsia stricta* is popular because it is easy to grow and because of its slender soft leaves and beautiful flowers. The flowering period is from spring to early summer. Small purple flowers peek out from the thick pink bract. After flowering, the plant produces pups for propagation. It does not tolerate dryness very well and should be misted three times per week.

● Growth pattern: Summer type
● Approximate size: 4in/10cm tall

## 2  Tillandsia bulbosa

Bromeliaceae Family, *Tillandsia* Genus

This plant is easily recognized by its bulbous form and wavy leaves. It likes water so do not forget to mist it. Place it in a spot that is well ventilated and does not receive direct sunlight. During its flowering cycle, it will form bright red bracts from which purple tubular flowers emerge.

● Growth pattern: Summer type
● Approximate size: 8–10in/20–25cm tall

## 3  Tillandsia tricolor var. melanocrater

Bromeliaceae Family, *Tillandsia* Genus

*Melanocrater* is a relative of the original species, *Tillandsia tricolor*. The name comes from how the inflorescence and flower petals have three colors—red, yellow and purple. *Melanocrater* differs from *Tillandsia tricolor* in that it is somewhat smaller and the inflorescences branch off during the flowering cycle. Give it sunlight and good ventilation. Take care that the base of the plant does not develop root rot.

● Growth pattern: Summer type
● Approximate size: 4–8in/10–20cm tall

## 4  Tillandsia fasciculata

Bromeliaceae Family, *Tillandsia* Genus

This large species of *Tillandsia* can grow three times larger than other species in both its diameter and height. The hard and sharp silver leaves spread out creating volume and a dynamic impression. They attach themselves to porous rocks or cacti to grow. *Tillandsia* fasciculate is robust and tough. This silver leaf variety needs plenty of sun.

● Growth pattern: Summer type
● Approximate size: 40in/1m tall at the
                 maximum

## 5  Tillandsia kolbii

Bromeliaceae Family, *Tillandsia* Genus

As *Tillandsia kolbii* looks very much like *Tillandsia ionantha* it is also known as *ionantha scarposa*. *Ionantha* leaves open up radially but *kolbii* curves in one direction. The flowers are tubular and pale purple in color. Water by misting twice a week.

● Growth pattern: Summer type
● Approximate size: 3in/7–8cm tall

## 6  Tillandsia harrisii

Bromeliaceae Family, *Tillandsia* Genus

This silver leaf variety is representative of the *Tillandsia* genus. The thickish silver leaves covered in trichome are beautiful. A strong stalk with red inflorescence grows up from the center of the plant and purple flowers bloom on it. The plant can be propagated by dividing. Display by hanging or planting it by itself in a terrarium.

● Growth pattern: Summer type
● Approximate size: 8in/20cm or more tall

### 1  *Pyrrhobryum dozyanum*

Rhizogoniaceae Family, *Rhizogonium* Genus

Also known in Japanese as Itachi-no-shippo (weasel's tail) because the soft fluffy leaves cover the stems, which are 2–4in/5–10cm long and stand up straight, look like the tail of some animal. The bright yellow-green colored mat of moss looks beautiful when the sun shines on it but when it is dry in winter, the moss will turn yellow so please keep it rehydrated.

### 2  *Leucobryum bowringii Mitt.*

Leucobryaceae Family *Leucobryum* Genus

Also known by the Japanese name of Manju-goke ("steamed bean-jam bun" moss) due to its fluffy, roundish and thick mat, it is used to cover the soil in pots of bonsai. When planting in pots, spread soil on top of a layer of compost made from broken down pieces of Japanese crypto-meria and cypress bark to ensure good drainage and so that the moss will be well ventilated.

### 3  *Polytrichum juniperinum*

Polytrichaceae Family, *Polytrichum* Genus

This is the type of moss most often used in Japanese-style moss gardens. Sunlight on this moss reveals its color and seems to make it shine. It has photosynthetic plates on the back of its leaves and can capture moisture from the air enabling it to avoid drying out. This moss does not need any special kind of care.

### 4  *Bartramia pomiformis*

Bartramiaceae Family, *Bartramia* Genus

This large moss is easily recognized by the round capsules which serve as spore cases. Its bright green color and delicate form are beautiful. When placed in a ter-rarium, it shows its attractive qualities. It is also possible to grow in a pot by plant-ing the seeds and germinating them.

## 1  *Brachymenium exile*

Bryaceae Family, *Brachymenium* Genus

This small type of moss grows densely in places with a sunny aspect including patches of soil or spaces in between asphalt in urban areas. It can be grown by tearing up a piece of it and replanting in a pot. It is quite robust and does not turn white when dried out. Does not need frequent watering.

## 2  *Thuidium*

Thuidiaceae Family, *Thuidium* Genus

*Thuidium* likes shaded parts of wetlands or on rocks, where it creeps horizontally to form flat colonies. The beautiful leaves are shaped like ferns. The leaves do not shrink when dry so it is suited to kokedama and terrariums. It is also fun to grow it by attaching it to driftwood or stones with crevices.

## 3  *Brachythecium plumosum*

Brachytheciaceae Family, *Brachythecium* Genus

As the stems branch off irregularly, this moss creeps and propagates, forming a thin mat. It is not very dense but it roots itself to the ground quite securely. It is easy to manage and one of the easiest mosses to look after. If the soil is dry when planting it, it will prevent the moss from germinating so give it plenty of water.

## 4  *Leucobryum juniperoideum*

Leucobryaceae Family *Leucobryum* Genus

This species of moss grows on the ground around the bottom of cryptomeria trees. The leaves are fairly thick and dense. The moss grows into a roundish mat and is well suited to bonsai. However, as it is quite dense, if watered too much it becomes too steamy and humid for the moss, making the color become whitish. Be careful of too much humidity.

## 5  *Marchantia polymorpha*

Marchantiaceae Family, *Marchantia* Genus

The thalli are difficult to distinguish as either roots, stems or leaves in this species. The structure of the cupules on the back of the leaves forms gemmae and this moss reproduces by releasing these gemmae into the surrounding environment. It likes damp places and puts down roots to attach itself securely as it crawls over the ground. If growing over a large area, it is difficult to remove.

## 1  Dicranales

Dicranaceae Family, <u>*Dicranum*</u> Genus

There are a few different species and each has different characteristics. On the whole, this moss is woolly and thick, giving a three dimensional effect. When growing it indoors, plant it rather deeply in leaf mold inside a container. Wet the surface with a spray once every two or three weeks and do not put it in get direct sunlight.

## 2  Hypnum plumaeforme Wilson

Hypnaceae Family, <u>*Hypnum*</u> Genus

This moss forms a large thick mat like a carpet, as its branches grow to the left and right. Tolerant of both dryness and damp-ness, it is fairly easy to grow. However, it does not like the heat and humidity of summer. Water generously from spring to summer, and manage by using shade nets or screens to block out the sun.

## 3  Conocephalum conicum

Conocephalaceae Family, <u>*Conocephalum*</u> Genus

The surface of the leaves looks like snake-skin, and in Japanese it is called Ja-goke (snake moss). There is also a smaller variety of this species. Its habitat is damp ground in mountainous areas and it has a particular smell, similar to *Houttuynia cordata*.

## 4  Pottiaceae

Pottiaceae Family, <u>*Hyophila*</u> Genus

Although the individual plant is small, this moss grows densely to form large col-onies. When it dries out the edges of the leaves curl completely inwards. The genus got its Japanese name Hamaki-goke (cigar moss) due to this phenomenon. If it turns brown, give it water and the leaves will turn green again.

## 5  Brachythecium populeum

Brachytheciaceae Family, <u>*Brachythecium*</u> Genus

This type of moss likes shade. The stems branch off irregularly as the plant creeps and grows, spreading out its mat. It roots itself to soil very strongly making it easy to use for kokedama or as undergrowth in the garden. So long as it is kept fairly damp, it grows without requiring too much care.

### 1  *Oncidium miltonia*

<u>Orchidaceae Family, Miltonia Genus</u>

Nearly 400 species of this orchid are distributed around Central and South America. The flowers all differ from one another and none of them have a distinct flowering period. Buds appear after new leaves have grown and a pseudobulb is formed. The newer bulbs can be divided off into new plants. If the leaves or bulbs take on a darker color, it means the orchid is not getting sufficient sunlight.

- <u>**Growth pattern:** Sympodial</u>
- <u>**Approximate size:** 4–28in/10–70cm</u>

### 4  *Dendrobium kingianum*

<u>Orchidaceae Family, *Dendrobium* Genus</u>

This is a small orchid native to Japan. The flower stem grows from the top of the bulb and contains many small flower buds on it. From when the buds begin to swell until the orchid has completely flowered, give it lots of water. The leaves can be sprayed with mist.

- <u>**Growth pattern:** Sympodial</u>
- <u>**Approximate size:** 6–20in/15–50cm tall</u>

### 2  *Angraecum didieri*

<u>Orchidaceae Family, *Angraecum* Genus</u>

At the end of a short flower stem which has leaves growing left and right alternately, blooms the white flower with a lovely fragrance. The small orchid originates from Madagascar. Although the plant itself is rather small, the flowers are fairly large and bloom at irregular intervals. It does not like cold so be careful of temperatures in winter. Replant once every three years.

- <u>**Growth pattern:** Monopodial</u>
- <u>**Approximate size:** 4–20in/10–50cm tall</u>

### 5  *Eria aporoides*

<u>Orchidaceae Family, *Eria* Genus</u>

This orchid is slightly unusual as it looks like a succulent with its dark green and fleshy leaves. In the flowering period, it bears several small white flowers bunched together on a spike. Even without flowers, this orchid can be enjoyed for its foliage.

- <u>**Growth pattern:** Monopodial</u>
- <u>**Approximate size:** 2–16in/5–40cm tall</u>

### 3  *Dendrobium* cv. Proud Appeal

<u>Orchidaceae Family, *Dendrobium* Genus</u>

Proud Appeal is a hybrid of *Dendrobium* cv. Formidible and *Dendrobium* cv. Midnight. The flowers are beautiful with their gradation from pink to purple, and they last for a long time. The plant itself is hardy and can be enjoyed for a long time. From early summer to autumn, reduce the amount of sunlight to 40% but the rest of the year, this plant can enjoy full sun.

- <u>**Growth pattern:** Sympodial</u>
- <u>**Approximate size:** 16–20in/40–50cm tall</u>

### 1  *Paphiopedilum*

Orchidaceae Family, *Paphiopedilum* Genus

This orchid is a terrestrial which grows in damp ground or on moss-covered rocks. As it does not have a bulb like many orchids, it dries out easily. When grown in a pot, this orchid needs pot mix that will be continually damp. Also, it does not like strong light and care must be taken to keep it shaded from direct sunlight all year round. It does not need much fertilizer.

- **Growth pattern:** Monopodial
- **Approximate size:** 8–40in/20cm–1m tall

### 2  *Masdevallia ignea*

Orchidaceae Family, *Masdevallia* Genus

This is a small type of orchid which grows wild in the Andes Mountains of South America. The sepals outside the petals of the flower have developed and given the orchid its unique shape. It is not tolerant of high temperatures making it somewhat difficult to grow. In summer spray it frequently with cold water to prevent the plant from weakening with the summer heat.

- **Growth pattern:** Sympodial
- **Approximate size:** 4–8in/10–20cm tall

### 3  *Midi phalaenopsis*

Orchidaceae Family, *Phalaenopsis* Genus

This orchid is a small type of *Phalaenopsis*. As well as being easy to display, the flowers last a long time. During summer, protect it from direct sunlight and from autumn to spring, keep it where it can get sun through a glass window. After flowers have finished blooming, if you cut the stem, a new flower stem will grow up from the node and the second round of orchids will flower.

- **Growth pattern:** Monopodial
- **Approximate size:** 6–20in/15–50cm tall

### 4  *Oncidium splendidum*

Orchidaceae Family, *Oncidium* Genus

This orchid is a perennial and native to Guatemala and Honduras. The panicle may reach a height of 1m. The orchids, which open on the end of the panicle, have slightly thick and large yellow flower petals. Too much moisture may cause root rot so it is better to keep it slightly dry aside from summer.

- **Growth pattern:** Sympodial
- **Approximate size:** 8–40in/20cm–1m tall

### 5  *Dendrochilum*

Orchidaceae Family, *Dendrochilum* Genus

On the long peduncle are two rows of greenish-yellow flowers, arranged in a regular fashion. The peduncle bends over like a bow. Manage in a bright and well ventilated place. After the flowers are finished, cut the plant at the base and replant it.

- **Growth pattern:** Sympodial
- **Approximate size:** 12–16in/30–40cm tall

### 6  *Dendrobium* cv. Angel Baby 'Green Ai'

Orchidaceae Family, *Dendrobium* Genus

This is a small orchid related to *Dendrobium nobile*. The combination of the dark green leaves and the numerous white flowers give it a pristine look. It should be replanted once every two or three years. If there are ten or more bulbs, the plant should be divided up. Spring is the time for both of these tasks.

- **Growth pattern:** Sympodial
- **Approximate size:** 4–28in/10–70cm tall

47 Beautiful Ideas Created with
Succulents, Air Plants, Moss and Orchids

# Decorative
# Terrariums

Published in 2018 by:
NIPPAN IPS Co., Ltd.
1-3-4 Yushima, Bunkyo-ku Tokyo,
113-0034, Japan

ISBN 978-4-86505-139-1

---

Photography: Yumiko Miyahama and Shinya Rachi

Author: Aya Kurosawa and Mika Miyoshi

Design: Ryo Takahashi

Editor: Mikinu Beppu (X-Knowledge)

Photography cooperation: ACME

Translation: Victoria Oyama
Thanks to TIME & SPACE, INC. for help with translation
http://www.timeandspace.jp

With the cooperation of:

Eisaku Ishikawa
Michikusa
http://www.y-michikusa.com/

Fumi Fujikawa
Species Nursery
http://speciesnursery.com

Toru Yamamoto
LLC Cactus Hirose

Takuya Sano
Sano Orchids
http://www.facebook.com/sanoorchids/

*TANIKU SHOKUBUTSU AIR PLANTS KOKE RAN DE TSUKURU
HAJIMETE NO TERRARIUMS*
© SUEKO KATSUJI 2016
Originally published in Japan in 2016 by X-Knowledge Co., Ltd.
English translation rights arranged with X-Knowledge Co., Ltd.

Printed in China